A Memoir of
Belle and Sebastian's Formative Year

IN THE ALL–NIGHT CAFÉ

Stuart David

PART ONE

Lisa Helps the Blind

1

One afternoon, in 1994, I had an idea.

It wasn't a particularly profound idea, or even an original one; I knew for certain that hundreds of people had had the same idea before me. But it came to me quite suddenly, quite out of the blue, and within a few weeks it had begun to change my life.

At that time, I was living in a small town on the west coast of Scotland called Alexandria, the place where I'd grown up. It lies twenty miles north of Glasgow, near the shores of Loch Lomond, and every afternoon when I needed a break from whatever song or story I was working on, I'd walk out of Alexandria and up into Balloch Park. I always took the same route: up the main drive, down the steep hill, through the arbour to the walled gardens and then home by the river. And it was while I was walking through the arbour, with the skinny trees twisting around and above me, that the idea came to me, almost as if it was spoken by a voice.

Initially, the idea presented itself as the solution to a

problem. For months we'd been auditioning bass players for my new band, Raglin Street Rattle. But everyone we tried seemed to be a frustrated lead guitarist rather than a bass player. Everyone wanted to play guitar, no one wanted to play bass. I was the singer and guitarist in the band, and as I walked along beneath the trees, it suddenly occurred to me that if I could learn to play the bass we could have our pick of guitar players. And that would be a blessing because I couldn't really play guitar very well.

I emerged from the arbour in a bit of a daze, trying to see if there was a flaw in the plan. I couldn't find one though. It didn't occur to me that I might not be able to play the bass. That didn't seem to be a possibility. So I hurried down through the walled gardens and out onto the path by the river, then I rushed home to phone my drummer and main collaborator, David Campbell, to tell him about the new plan.

I was twenty-four years old the afternoon the idea came to me, and for a while there had been a major threat to my way of life looming on the horizon. Like most people who came to prominence during the Britpop and BritArt era, I'd been funding my musical apprenticeship using Unemployment Benefit (or more specifically, Income Support), using it as an unofficial artist's bursary in the absence of anything more legitimate. But now the government were beginning to crack down on the various misuses to which their £46 a week was being put, and I knew I was on thin ice. They were herding everyone who had been claiming benefits for more than a year onto Training For Work programmes, and then into invented jobs—and I'd been claiming for almost eight years, ever since a Modern Studies teacher had given us a brief lesson in how to sign on and attend school at the same time. So I knew my time was running out.

My drummer, David Campbell, had found a solution that was working for him. In order to fund his regular American road trips, he'd given up his benefits altogether and enrolled in a scheme at the hospital to have medical experiments carried out on himself; he only had to take part in a study for about one week every couple of months to make enough money to get by. But I was pretty certain I didn't have the stomach for that. So I'd been filling in my Looking For Work diaries, attending enforced meetings with assessors, and one unhappy Tuesday morning I found myself sitting in a cramped boardroom with ten or fifteen fellow claimants, being shown by an enthusiastic man with a flipchart how to look for work.

The irony of the situation, the fact that he didn't appear to have anything you could seriously call a job himself, wasn't lost on the party, but it didn't really matter. It turned out that we hadn't been gathered there to be taught how to look for work at all. Towards the end of the morning, he brought out a folder and started passing bits of paper around, and it seemed this was the real business of the day. We were told to look down the list of courses typed on the sheets of paper, and then choose one we'd like to sign up for, otherwise our benefits would be stopped.

My heart sank. I scanned the sorry list of options, wondering how I could rearrange things to get by without my £46 a week. Ever since I'd turned fourteen, I'd been convinced that writing songs and stories was my vocation. I considered my work to be similar in nature to a religious calling, and I'd dedicated myself to it accordingly. No other possibilities existed for me. I'd always just refused to consider anything else. But I'd only been able to win the ensuing teenage battles about my career choice with teachers and family and peers because Income Support had given me a modicum of financial independence. My benefits had allowed me to follow my own path, despite what anyone else said. Without the benefits, I knew I'd be fair game again for the factories in the valley and the nuclear missile base on the other side of the hill: the twin evils I'd been born and raised to provide cheap labour for, just like everyone else in Alexandria.

I looked down the list of courses again, even more desperately this time, and it remained a sorry selection: flower arranging, dog grooming, car mechanics. But then, just when I was on the verge of giving up all hope, something seemed to materialise near the bottom of the page—a late addition, in tiny writing. A course in Glasgow that appeared to have something to do with popular music. I thought I might be hallucinating. I called the flipchart man over and asked him about it. He took the piece of paper from me and stood staring at it blankly.

'Hmn…' he said after a while. 'I didn't know that was on there. That sounds strange.'

Then he wrote my name down, said he would look into it for me and sent us all home.

For a few weeks I didn't hear anything more about it, and after a while I decided I must just have imagined the words onto the page through sheer force of will. I forgot about it, borrowed the money to buy a Fender Squier bass, and started taking lessons at a youth club in the next town along from mine, on Tuesday and Thursday nights. It wasn't until I got called into the unemployment offices again and asked what I intended to do about this new deal of theirs that I mentioned the music course I had heard about.

The woman behind the desk looked at me uncomprehendingly. She studied her notes and said there wasn't a music course, then she tried to get me to choose from one of the other courses she suggested. I told her there had been a music course on the list at the Looking For Work seminar, and that it was based in Glasgow. She eyed me suspiciously, studied her notes again, then told me I'd be hearing from them in due course regarding a decision about my benefit.

That seemed to be the end of the interview.

A few days later, though, I got a letter saying an appointment had been set up for me at an unemployment office in Glasgow, and when I arrived there it turned out that the music course existed after all.

The harassed-looking man who interviewed me said the course was called Beatbox. And although I thought the name was daft, I liked the sound of some of the things it had to offer.

'If you sign up for it,' the interviewer told me, 'you'll receive an extra £10 a week on top of your normal benefits, plus a travel allowance.'

I certainly liked the sound of that, but there were other things I liked the sound of too. I particularly liked that the course had its own recording studio. I thought I would probably be able to record my new band in there.

'Do they teach music?' I asked. 'Will I be able to learn to play the bass guitar there?'

The interviewer said he thought I probably would, so I told him I'd like to sign up.

He nodded.

'There's just one problem at the moment,' he said. 'The course is moving to new, better premises so it'll be a few weeks before you can start.'

I told him that was fine, and he nodded again, then he went to work on trying to find some forms for me amongst the carnage on his desk, and I sat and filled them in—one by one—till the daylight was fading away.

2

Getting out of Alexandria on the train, and heading for Glasgow, had always been something I'd done as often as I could afford to. And I was looking forward to having a travel pass that allowed me to do it every day now. A few years earlier I'd read an article in *The Glasgow Herald* by a journalist following the campaign trail for the 1992 General Election, which had described the journey in the opposite direction.

'We trundled through Garscadden and Clydebank,' he wrote, 'passing all the gap sites Hitler and Thatcher left behind… I hail a taxi and head into Alexandria. Alexandria is a dump. Half the town is broken, demolished, vandalised, neglected or concrete. I wander nervously through the shopping arcade; this urban-jungle horror, like Keith Waterhouse's Brighton, looks like a town helping the police with their enquiries.'

So going the other way always meant going in the right direction. Glasgow shone like a beacon for me. It was a place of grandeur and leafy streets, sandstone buildings and a vibrant energy. I began to wonder if Beatbox would be in one of those grand buildings, hidden down one of those leafy lanes. But I was in for a surprise.

I don't know where Beatbox's original premises were, but if the new venue was a step up I felt grateful, on my first day there, that I'd come on board at this particular point in time and not any earlier. The whole operation was housed beneath a slip road that ran up to a business park in Finnieston, and the slip road itself formed the roof of the building. There were no windows in the concrete walls, just a single metal door at the top of a short flight of stairs. As I pushed the heavy door open and stumbled inside, I felt as if I was entering a strange subterranean labyrinth, or an underground bunker built to withstand a nuclear blast.

I'd pretty much decided halfway through my first day that I wouldn't go back to Beatbox again. From what I could tell, the course was a total shambles. Just scores of unemployed musicians sitting around in a dark, airless labyrinth, doing nothing. No one seemed to be in charge. There was a music computer room with five or six Atari STs, which mostly seemed to be for playing computer golf on. There was a songwriting room with a digital piano and about forty empty chairs in it. And then there was the recording studio, which comprised a live room where the temperature was five or six degrees below zero, and a control room whose door was firmly locked. Apart from that, there was an L-shaped communal area surrounding the main office—which was also firmly locked—and a long dark corridor which connected all the other dark rooms together, where most of the musicians on the course were sprawled out on dilapidated sofas, or sitting on the floor with their backs against the wall.

I wandered around on my own, trying to work out what was what, while people scowled at me, or just stared blankly into space. A thick cloud of cigarette smoke pervaded the place, and something about the absence of daylight and the lack of fresh air made me wonder if the place was actually a detention centre set up by the government to incarcerate all the people they'd caught using Social Security benefit as an arts bursary. It seemed possible, judging by the forlorn look in most of the inmates' eyes.

One thing that particularly intrigued me, though, as I wandered around, was the poster which hung on at least one wall of every room I went into.

It was a poster of a band, but a band I'd never heard of and they looked like a cross between The Commitments and Take That, if such a cross is possible. There were seven or eight of them in the photograph, most prominently a woman with pineapple hair who had a saxophone strapped around her neck, and a guy in a vest who was lying on the floor in front of them all, propped up on one elbow, staring seductively into the camera. I wondered if they were a real band, or if the poster was a fake, rigged up to give the detention centre the illusion of being a music course for the benefit of the inmates.

Time dragged. All day, nothing happened. No one played any music, no one even picked up an instrument and held it just to pose. There didn't seem to be any musical instruments anywhere in the whole building, except for a drum kit with no hi-hats and no cymbals in a corner of the freezing-cold live room. I started to think the day would never end, but then, late in the afternoon, a woman came out of the main office and called me and two or three other people who had started the course that day into the studio control room. I instantly recognised her as the person holding a saxophone in the band poster plastered on the walls.

The control room actually looked quite impressive compared to everything else I had seen so far. There was a sixteen-track desk, a tower of outboard effects equipment, two eight-track recording machines and a million wires and cables.

As we sat down, the woman with the pineapple hair apologised for the disorganised state of the course.

'We've just moved into this new building,' she said. 'We're still trying to get things sorted.'

Then she told us a little bit about what we'd be doing on the course and asked us what we'd like to get out of it.

I said I'd like to learn to play the bass guitar. She pointed to two guys in the corner and said they could probably teach me. One was called Kris and the other one was called Happy. I asked them how long they thought it would take me to learn.

'It depends how good you want to be,' Kris said. 'Some things could take you a lifetime to master, but you'll probably be as good as Bill Wyman in about six months, if you practise enough.'

Good enough to play in The Rolling Stones by the spring! That sounded perfect. So despite the lack of daylight, despite the fog of cigarette smoke and the general air of doom that hung alongside it in the corridors, I decided to go back again the next day.

And I kept on going.

The first real friend I made at Beatbox was a guy called Alistair, who played guitar and wore a pork-pie hat. Looking back, I think it might be possible that our friendship was born out of a misunderstanding, although I'm not entirely sure. Alistair was interested in S&M, and it occurs to me now that the first time we struck up a conversation I was wearing a pair of leather trousers. He said something about them which I didn't quite catch, but it seems possible that, because of the trousers, he mistakenly thought I shared his interest. Still, once we got talking it became clear we had quite a lot in common. We both wrote our own songs, we were both looking for something to happen and we both had the feeling that things in Beatbox weren't quite as they should be.

My first impressions of the place hadn't been too far wide of the mark: the whole set-up was definitely something of a shambles.

We did get the occasional lesson in one thing or another. We learned how to use Cubase, a music sequencing program, on the Atari ST computers, and there were sporadic singing lessons and classes in how to use the mixing desk, on the rare occasions when the studio door wasn't locked. We were sometimes herded into the room with the digital piano for what were called songwriting lessons, but were really just sessions of people playing songs they'd written, followed by the tutor telling us why they were good. But those bursts of activity were exceptions rather than the norm, and on top of that it had quickly become clear to me that all the band members on that poster that hung in every room were either tutors on the course, or administrators in the office. When the studio door was locked it was very often them who were in there.

'They're squandering our talents,' Alistair said. 'They don't even know what they've got here.'

So he'd decided to take matters into his own hands, to see Beatbox mainly as a resource for bringing a lot of disparate musicians together, and to try and make something happen for himself. He started out by suggesting we should do a bit of work on each other's songs and to try to get them recorded.

By then, I was beginning to get somewhere with the bass. My promised lessons in Beatbox had been infrequent and haphazard, and the bass guitar they had in the studio terrified me.

'This is how you turn it on,' the tutor had said during my first lesson. I'd never come across a guitar you had to turn on before. He flicked a switch on the body and a small red light began to glow.

'Active pickups,' he explained. He turned the bass round and showed me the back of it. 'The batteries go in here,' he said, pointing at a big plastic compartment.

'What are active pickups for?' I asked him.

He leant towards me, grinning maniacally.

'To make it growl like a bastard,' he said. He turned the volume up on the amplifier and started playing some complicated funk. The amplifier growled like a bastard. Then he adjusted some switches and knobs on the bass, and started slapping the strings like Mark King from Level 42.

I'd given up going along to the youth club for bass lessons on Tuesday and Thursday nights too. But, in the meantime, I'd discovered something which had turned out to be a revelation for me: tutorials on VHS—videotapes where men with dubious moustaches and heavily patterned shirts ran you through all the ins and outs of the instrument and how to play it, in segments you could rewind and pause and repeat until you had them mastered. And despite the moustaches and the faint air of menace, they were working out for me. After a couple of months' practice, I'd got good enough to start rehearsing with David Campbell in preparation for auditioning guitarists for Raglin Street Rattle, and I'd also decided to start playing with as many people as I could at Beatbox, just to try and get the hang of the thing. So Alistair's idea that we start playing together had come just at the right time.

3

Alistair lived in a basement flat on Otago Street in the west end of Glasgow, and one afternoon he invited me round there to play bass on some of his songs, and to give him the chance to work out the guitar for a couple of mine. The idea of escaping Beatbox's foggy darkness for a while was always appealing, and the west end of Glasgow was an enchanted and alien place to me back then, the centre of a bohemian culture far removed from the world I'd grown up in. So I quickly agreed.

When we made the arrangement, I thought it was just going to be the two of us working together, but when I arrived there was someone else I recognised from Beatbox sitting in the kitchen too. He was holding an acoustic guitar, drinking from one of Alistair's brightly coloured mugs, and I remembered we'd had a singing lesson together in the freezing-cold live room of the Beatbox studio. We'd never really spoken before, though, and as I sat down at the table in front of a colourful mug of my own, Alistair introduced us.

'Stuart,' he said, to neither of us in particular, 'this is Stuart.'

I got the feeling that the other Stuart hadn't expected anyone else to be there either, and that he'd probably come round expecting to be working with Alistair on his own too. We nodded at each other and mentioned the singing lesson we'd done in Beatbox. Then I remembered Stuart had blushed when the focus was on him at one point during the lesson, which had made me think he was shy like me. He'd been wearing a woollen jumper with a picture of a teddy bear on the front, and his DIY haircut and retro aesthetic had reminded me of Stephen from The Pastels, who my friend Karn was a big fan of. I'd understood straight away the world Stuart was from, but I hadn't heard any of his own songs before that afternoon at Alistair's.

Alistair seemed to have some kind of songwriter's circle in mind now that we were all there, so we passed the acoustic guitar round the kitchen table and took turns to sing one of our own songs. We talked a bit about the state of Beatbox too, and swapped theories as to why we thought it was the way it was. And now and again Alistair would say,

'I really need to show you both my dungeon after this. I think you're really going to like my dungeon', provoking one of us to start up another song in the hope that we wouldn't find out what he was talking about.

Alistair played a song called 'Planet of the Apes'; Stuart played one called 'Melanie Voodoo'. I played one I'd written recently with David Campbell called 'Where Did You Go?'. I thought my friend Karn would like Stuart's songs. They sounded a bit like the songs she sometimes sent to me on mixtapes—The Pastels, The BMX Bandits, Wire. And I told Stuart he was lucky because there already seemed to be an audience for the kind of thing he was doing. I don't know if he took too kindly to that comment, but at least it kept Alistair off the subject of his dungeon for a little bit longer.

I'm still not entirely sure what Alistair had in mind when he invited us both round like that. Stuart always wore quite a big pair of boots at that time, and he also had some unusual trousers, so it's quite possible Alistair had made the same S&M mistake he'd made with me.

Either way, when neither me nor Stuart had any songs left to sing, Alistair started grinning in excitement, and ceremoniously led us out into the hallway, where he opened a door that revealed a narrow stone staircase disappearing down into the darkness. Stuart and I looked at each other with a combination of trepidation and bemusement, then Alistair clicked on the light switch and told us to follow him down.

It was a tight squeeze, but at the bottom of the staircase we were suddenly in a large empty space, underground, a single light bulb hanging in the middle of the ceiling and brown stone tiles covering the walls and the floor. It felt a bit like being inside a cave, but a very disturbing cave, where the tiled floor sloped in four sections towards a drain in the middle, and chains and handcuffs and leather shackles hung on the walls.

'What do you think?' Alistair asked us, chuckling enthusiastically. 'I do a lot of photography down here. Dominatrixes, masochists, leather freaks. Things like that. What do you think?'

Neither of us spoke. We stared at each other and raised our eyebrows. Alistair asked us again what we thought. We remained silent.

'Can we go back upstairs now?' Stuart said eventually, and I lent my support to that suggestion.

'Really?' Alistair said, and he seemed quite crestfallen, but we both nodded and headed for the tight little staircase. We agreed to meet up again soon, and to play some stuff on each other's songs to see where it would go, but we didn't go anywhere near the basement again.

Around the same time that I started playing with Stuart and Alistair, David Campbell and I also found a guitarist for our own band. It had been a long search. Raglin Street Rattle was going to be our third band together. I had a strong vision for it, and we'd been working on making that vision a reality for almost a year.

I'd met David five years earlier, on a brief Electronic Music Recording course at a college for bricklayers and joiners in Clydebank. Like me, David had planned to escape the place he'd grown up in via music, and like me his plans had stalled. The place David was trying to escape from was Glasgow's sprawling council estate, Easterhouse, deprived of even the factories and missile base that Alexandria had as options. The only real career opportunity in Easterhouse was signing on—and David was still there, having done that—and now taking part in the clinical drug trials that funded his trips to America.

David was six years older than me, and in the two

bands we'd formed since meeting at college I'd been the singer and songwriter and David had played drums. At the same time he'd been writing and recording his own songs, sending them off to London, getting the same rejection letters back as me. But for this new band we'd been writing together, collaborating more fully. And once I'd decided to switch to bass, we'd auditioned a steady string of guitarists who'd responded to the adverts we'd been posting in music shops in Glasgow, asking for people who were influenced by Tom Waits and The Waterboys and Bob Dylan.

When we auditioned Diane we knew she had the sound we'd been looking for—and we thought maybe this time we'd get out of the towns that had trapped us.

Coincidentally, both my own band, and the thing I was doing with Stuart and Alistair, had set their sights on the same initial goal. We were both rehearsing our way towards the same first step—a spot on the open mic stage at The Halt Bar on Saturday afternoons. But although both bands were working towards the same thing, the way each one went about it was very different.

At Alistair's, we usually rehearsed in his front room. The walls were painted yellow and the woodwork was painted red. Even now, those colours are bright in my memory. Very bright. Alistair was the main driving force for the project at that time. Not for the writing of the songs, but for continuing to get us together, and for pushing us forward to rehearse for some live appearances. Alistair was older than us, although we didn't know that to begin with. I was twenty-four, Stuart was a year and a half older and Alistair was forty-two. He didn't look it. He had a shaved head and a goatee beard and after a while he told us that some of his body had been rebuilt with metal pins after a bad motorbike accident. He only ever took his pork-pie hat off when we were rehearsing, and then he sometimes took his shirt off too and watched himself in the mirror. He had some dressmaker's mannequins, naked and with various limbs missing, in his living room, which made for quite an unsettling audience.

We were rehearsing three songs for The Halt Bar. One by each of us. We all took lead vocals on the song we'd written and swapped the instruments around, using a drum machine to stay in time. Alistair's song was 'Planet of the Apes', mine was one I'd written with David called 'On Brilliant Wings'. Stuart's was called 'Le Pastie de la Bourgeoisie'. He'd written it after seeing some graffiti on the wall of Gregg's the bakers that said the same thing, and he'd written a twangy lead guitar part like Duane Eddy for Alistair to play. We rehearsed now and again for a few weeks, but Alistair was keen to get us out playing live as quickly as possible.

Practising with David and Diane as Raglin Street Rattle was quite a different situation. We always hired a rehearsal studio and played with the live drum kit. And everyone always kept their shirt on.

But in contrast to Alistair pushing me and Stuart to get out playing live as soon as possible, Diane was insisting on rehearsing and rehearsing and rehearsing, convinced we were nowhere near ready to play in public. David and I had been practising together for months before Diane joined, getting the rhythm section as tight as possible, and I'd finally got the hang of playing the bass and singing at the same time, even though it had felt like rubbing your stomach with one hand and tapping your head with the other for quite a while. Diane's guitar parts sounded perfect to us now, and as far as we were concerned we were ready to go. Certainly ready to do a few songs in The Halt Bar. But Diane wanted to rehearse some more.

And some more.

So the project with Stuart and Alistair got to The Halt Bar first.

There were a few places scattered around the city where singer-songwriters could turn up and do open mic spots. They all took place on different days of the week. On Monday nights, there was The Star Folk Club in the Society of Musicians building on Berkeley Street. Tuesday evenings, it was The Glasgow Songwriters, downstairs in Blackfriars in the Merchant City. Open mics at The Halt Bar took place on Wednesday nights and Saturday afternoons, and Alistair decided we should make our debut there on a Saturday, because there was usually less drinking and a more discerning crowd through the day.

'Maybe it would be better if the audience is drunk,' I said. But Alistair insisted that there wouldn't be any mistakes.

We met up at his flat on the Saturday between Christmas and New Year, and walked to the bar together, freezing cold, down Gibson Street and then along Woodlands Road. I'd done regular open mic spots at Blackfriars and the Society of Musicians in the past, but I'd never played in The Halt before. I often went along to watch with a couple of friends, but the sessions were made up of a core group of regulars who all seemed to know each other, and I'd always been too shy to ask if I could go on and do some songs. Alistair knew a lot of the regulars; he'd been in a band called Van Daal until recently, and they'd often played at The Halt Bar.

'It's all set,' he'd told me the day before in Beatbox. 'I've warned them in advance we're coming.'

We didn't take any instruments with us. Everyone always shared what was there—most of the equipment belonged to the house band, The Moondials, and as we walked along I hoped the bass wouldn't have an active pickup. This was going to be my first time playing bass in public, and I didn't want it to growl at anyone.

'We're ready for this,' Alistair said as he pushed the door of the bar open, and I felt my stomach fluttering. The heat of the bar came out to meet us, and we stepped into a low cloud of cigarette smoke, similar to the one that hung permanently in Beatbox, but with the added smell of stale beer lingering beneath it.

There were two rooms in The Halt. In the public bar, the broad, frosted windows flooded the space with daylight, and an oval-shaped bar sat like an island in the middle of the large room. Live music took place in the lounge bar, a smaller and darker place, with the bar running down one wall until it met a triangular stage at the end. Both rooms were traditional and ornate, with wooden fixtures and glass panels. There was an alcove with a leather bench at the back of the lounge bar where you could always get a good view of the stage. I tried to sit there when I came with my friends.

They were still setting up the PA when we arrived, and Alistair went to talk to the compère to see if we could get on early. Everything had usually already started when I arrived and it was strange to get this glimpse behind the scenes. I bought us Cokes and sat with Stuart on the leather bench at the back, watching as they dragged the bass drum with The Moondials' logo emblazoned on it up the short flight of stairs at the front of the stage and soundchecked the PA.

'They'll put us on second or third,' Alistair said when he returned. He was keen not to have to sit through too many of the other acts. 'We'll get on and get out,' he said.

The Halt sessions were compèred by Sandy Nelson, a songwriter who always started off by singing a song or two of his own. After Sandy had got things going, he'd start to draw on the pool of regulars he called The Usual Suspects—which included Helen Reeves, a guy called Brendan who looked like Mickey Rourke and The Moondials themselves—in various combinations, or all together.

The Moondials were a traditional R 'n' B band, like the early Rolling Stones. On the rare occasions when Sandy was absent, their guitarist, Stevie Jackson, would compère instead, asking the audience for requests between acts, and seemingly able to play anything that anyone asked for. And their singer Warren sounded like Joe Cocker and looked like Johnny Depp. I sometimes thought that if I looked like Warren, I would feel more confident onstage. And that I would maybe have been a pop star already. I couldn't work out why Warren wasn't a pop star already.

None of the open mic sessions I went to ever had a fixed running order. If you were there to do a song the compère would never tell you when you'd be on, or who you'd follow. They did it all in the moment, judging by the current performance what they thought would work best next; like a DJ improvising a set by gauging the mood of the room. Sometimes, in The Star Folk Club, the compère, Arthur Johnstone, would walk amongst the tables while the singer onstage was coming to an end of their song and tap me on the shoulder, whispering in my ear,

'I'll put you on next.'

I'd seen Sandy do that occasionally too. But most of the time you'd just realise suddenly during one of the introductions that it was leading up to your own name, and your stomach would lurch. Sitting through each act meant trying not to think if you'd be on after them, and every introduction was another few seconds of the ground disappearing beneath you while you half hoped for a reprieve—just one more song by someone else— and half hoped it was your turn now, to get it all over with.

'It must be us soon,' Alistair said when Brendan finished. But there were a couple of more introductions and a couple of more songs before I finally heard Sandy saying the words—'three new songwriters who haven't played together before'—amongst a bunch of other things, and we made our way across the bar and up the little flight of stairs at the front of the stage.

Sandy helped us on with the guitars and adjusted the mic stands to the right height. I couldn't believe how heavy the bass was; the fretboard felt like a tree trunk in my hand. But I was glad to find no switch or batteries for the pickup.

'Stuart, Stuart and Alistair,' Sandy said, and there was a smattering of applause. Then Alistair stepped up to the lead microphone and we played 'Planet of the Apes'. It was scrappy. We were all over the place without the drum machine, but Alistair danced and thankfully the shirt stayed on. Then we swapped instruments and I found myself with the acoustic guitar. I moved to the lead microphone and sang 'On Brilliant Wings', grateful for a rest from the hulking bass, and the way my fingers seemed barely to move on its unvarnished fretboard. Now that I was at the front I could see that nothing really mattered too much. There was hardly anybody in the audience, and some of the few who were there were sitting facing away from the stage. No one facing us was watching with any great scrutiny, and I imagined most of them were just doing the stomach lurch, wondering if they'd be on next. I looked at a few people and felt glad I wasn't still out there waiting with them, that I was up here getting it over with.

Stuart and Alistair were both out of time with what I was singing, my guitar sounded scratchy, the bass hit a wrong note, my voice sounded like it was coming through a loud telephone, far away—but I had my plans with David Campbell; other plans. I thought about how things would sound when he got back from his current American road trip, and then we came to the end of the song and I returned to the task of trying to support the weight of the killer bass again.

Two handrails rose up on either side of the short

flight of steps, and at the top of the steps they continued on around the stage, one in each direction, so that it seemed the stage was separated from the rest of the bar by a garden fence. I leant on the section in front of me, letting it take some of the weight of the bass, while Alistair adjusted the mic stand for Stuart, and Stuart altered the length of the guitar strap. Then Alistair said,

'This is "La Pastie de la Bourgeoisie".'

He counted us in, and we started—Alistair dancing more enthusiastically than ever as he played the twanging lead guitar introduction. We were out of time, all faster than usual, and Stuart sang the opening lines and then stopped. The whole thing slowly clattered to a halt.

'Sorry,' Stuart said. 'I can't hear myself. Can someone turn the mic up?'

Gary from The Moondials came up and fiddled with the mixing desk. There was a squall of feedback and he twisted some more knobs.

'Try that,' he said, and Stuart made a popping sound into the microphone. He didn't look very convinced.

'Let's go,' Alastair said, and he counted us in again. He twanged the intro with even more enthusiasm than before, dancing as hard as he could, and after the same couple of lines Stuart stopped singing again. Then stopped strumming.

'Sorry,' he said. Alistair reached over and started adjusting Stuart's microphone stand, but Stuart had already taken the guitar off.

'Sorry,' he said again. 'I can't do it.'

Sandy was standing down at the front, looking up at us. He waited to see what would happen, and then he shrugged.

'Is that it?' he asked, and then he came up the steps.

'I think that's it,' he said into the microphone, as Stuart handed him the guitar. 'Stuart, Stuart and Alistair.'

Stuart was the first down the steps and there was some applause.

'That sounded like a good song,' Sandy said. 'I liked your voice,' he said to Stuart, and Alistair finally seemed to realise that Stuart wasn't coming back. I took the bass off and felt my shoulder floating up towards the ceiling, free at last of the punishing weight. I went down the stairs while Alistair was still taking off his guitar and sat up on the back bench beside Stuart.

'What happened?' I asked him.

He shrugged. 'It didn't feel right,' he said.

Sandy introduced Helen Reeves, and she climbed up the steps and took her own turn of the guitar. I watched Alistair milling around, wondering if he could manage to convince anyone that he didn't actually know us. Eventually he came and sat down beside us. When Helen finished her first song he said, 'Come on, let's get out of here. Let's go.'

We let him stand outside on his own for a while and then followed him, back out into the cold, just as Sandy was introducing Electric Anderson.

On the train home, I thought of a performance I'd once seen Electric Anderson do in The Halt; a near ten-minute acoustic version of Bob Dylan's 'Knockin' on Heaven's Door'. Sandy always struggled to keep Electric's spots to the allotted time, sometimes just having to climb up onto the stage and ask for a round of applause during the thirteenth verse of something. But around the six-minute mark of this particular performance of 'Knockin' on Heaven's Door', a minor miracle had occurred. Standing too close to the microphone, Electric Anderson had bumped against it, sending an amplified thump echoing around the room, and at the same time knocking his false teeth out. He'd felt them falling, reached up mid-strum, swiftly dropped them into his jacket pocket without missing a beat of the song and then carried on toothless for another three or four minutes as if nothing had happened.

I laughed, looking out the train window, and wondered if he'd finished today's set yet. I was only at Clydebank, half an hour out of Glasgow. It was possible Sandy was just about to climb onto the stage, any minute now, to bring the curtain down on a marathon version of 'It Ain't Me, Babe'.

4

Soon after our Halt Bar appearance, we started getting together round at Alistair's place to focus exclusively on playing Stuart's songs. By then, my own band was doing my songs the way I wanted them to sound, and I didn't feel the need to play them with Stuart and Alistair any more. I can't remember why we stopped playing Alistair's songs. But Stuart was writing a huge amount during that period, and he had no one else to play his songs with. He liked the way Alistair could make his lead parts twang, and he liked the way I played single root notes on the bass, so we gradually got together just to play his songs, with Stuart as the singer. And we soon had a few songs that were ready to record.

The rule at Beatbox was that, after you had been on the course for six weeks, you were entitled to one day in the studio every month to record your own material. Like most things at Beatbox, though, the rule existed purely in the abstract. Gordon Rintoul, the head of

Beatbox, was also the manager of the band in the posters on the walls, and—convinced of their imminent stardom—he was forever altering the recording schedule for the studio to finish off the band's latest demo. As a result, the diary was so backed up with cancelled sessions and reshuffled assignments that getting your day in there was almost impossible. So we decided to take a DIY approach.

In 1995, it still wasn't possible to record much audio on a computer. Home PCs weren't big enough or fast enough, and the Atari STs we used in the music computer room were solely for sequencing MIDI data. But in my attic at home I had a four-track cassette recorder, a reverb unit and a blue plastic microphone. I'd been getting quite good results with it, using some of the techniques I'd learned on my Electronic Music Recording course. So, when we were ready, I invited Stuart and Alistair up to Alexandria to record a few songs there.

It was a tight fit. The attic I lived in was long and narrow, with walls that sloped towards the ceiling, and you could only really stand up straight in the middle of the room. With the bed at one end and a low table at the other, though, there wasn't really a spot where we could all stand up at once, so we crouched down over the four-track, constantly bumping each other with our guitars, and we got to work.

There was only one headphone socket on the four-track, and I only had one pair of headphones anyway, so Stuart wore them to hear himself singing, while me and Alistair tried to keep in time with the jangle of the unamplified guitars. It wasn't easy, but we managed to record four songs: 'The Disenchanted Pony', 'Your Secrets', 'Melanie Voodoo' and 'La Pastie de la Bourgeoisie'. Now and again we had to stop when the neighbour's lawnmower started bleeding onto the vocal track, but once we'd added some reverb and bounced the mixes down onto a chrome cassette we were pretty happy with the results.

Stuart made some copies, and on the cassette labels he wrote the band name, 'Lisa Helps the Blind', after an article he'd recently read in the newspaper. It was only supposed to be the name for those recordings initially, but because we were slowly morphing into a band, it's what we came to be called.

And meanwhile, Diane kept Raglin Street Rattle rehearsing.

And rehearsing.

Diane and Alistair never met, but there seemed to be a certain symbiotic relationship between them. A law of inverse proportion. The more Diane procrastinated, the harder Alistair pushed Lisa Helps the Blind. The more Diane wanted us to rehearse, the more Alistair wanted us to be out there, getting on with things.

'You and Stuart are both still young,' he told me one day, while we were sitting up against the corridor wall in Beatbox. 'Time's running out for me. If I don't make it soon, I won't make it at all.'

He was frustrated at the speed Stuart wanted to do things, but there was a reason why Stuart was taking things so slowly. For the past five or six years he'd been suffering from chronic fatigue syndrome. It had overtaken him while he'd been studying physics at

Glasgow University, and although he was slowly getting better, he just didn't have the energy to move at the pace Alistair was hoping for.

'It's frustrating the hell out of me,' Alistair said, and he booked us a gig at the opening of an art exhibition; something he said would start to get us noticed.

Stuart would probably have preferred to work on a few more recordings rather than get out playing live at that stage. He'd spent some time making covers from collages of photocopied images for the cassette we'd already recorded, and sometimes he spent rehearsals putting posters and press packages together. But he accepted Alistair's insistence that we play the gig with good grace, and we settled into an accelerated rehearsal schedule, once again under the ever-watchful gaze of the naked and deformed dressmaker's dummies.

One thing Stuart did resist Alistair on was the use of the drum machine. I love early drum machines, but this was a horrendous thing: a big flat slab of black plastic that sounded exactly as if Stock, Aitken and Waterman had thrown it out a few years before.

'Not with the drum machine,' Stuart was always saying, at the start of each rehearsal.

'It's the only way to stay in time,' Alistair would tell him.

'We don't need to stay in time,' Stuart would reply, and Alistair would take his shirt off and reluctantly do a few songs without the beats, his expression in the mirror growing ever more frustrated. Then, eventually, he'd hit the play button on the boombox at the start of another run-through, and the whole thing would kick off again.

We did manage to convince him, though, not to

37

bring it along to the art gallery on the night of the gig. It wasn't easy, but we got through to him in the end.

'We're going to look like amateurs,' he told us, but that was better than sounding like Rick Astley.

Neither me nor Stuart knew exactly where the art gallery was, so we met round at Alistair's. He'd booked a taxi to take us there with our guitars and two little practice amps. We stood out on his front step waiting for the taxi to arrive, listening to the birds chirping in the fading daylight, full of expectation.

'We're ready for this,' Alistair said. 'It's going to be a good one.'

But it wasn't. And as soon as we arrived at the gallery it was clear that it wouldn't be. For a start, the woman in charge of the event didn't have the first clue who Alistair was.

'I arranged it all with Caroline,' he told her. 'She asked us to come along and perform tonight.'

'Caroline isn't here,' the woman said. 'She didn't tell me anything about it.'

'Can you contact her?' Alistair asked, and the woman shook her head. A man in a white shirt and a black tie came and stood beside her.

'Do you know anything about this?' the woman asked him.

'About what?' he said.

'Some band.'

The man shook his head and wandered off again.

'It was all arranged,' Alistair said, and the woman started to look annoyed. 'What if we just set up over there?' he asked her, pointing towards the corner. She didn't say anything for a minute, then she sighed loudly and shrugged.

'Come on,' Alistair said to us, and he led the way across the room.

People were starting to arrive by then. The room was filling up with corporate people who made a beeline for the wine table and then stood in groups with their backs to the art on the walls. We put our amps down in the corner and started to unpack our guitars.

'Crap,' Alistair said when he'd folded up the bin bag he used for a guitar case, and we looked at him. 'There's nowhere to plug in,' he said.

The woman in charge walked past and Alistair pointed out the problem to her.

'Is there somewhere we can run a cable from?' he asked.

'There aren't any sockets you can use,' she told him, then she wandered off again.

He looked kind of stunned for a few minutes, then he pulled himself together.

'We're just going to have to do it acoustic,' he told us.

We weren't convinced. Stuart thought we should just go home. We'd been under the impression there would be a vocal PA for Stuart to sing through, and we didn't see how we could do it acoustically with an electric guitar and electric bass. But Alistair insisted. He told us to tune up and then he counted us in.

I could hear Stuart's acoustic guitar, but I couldn't hear his singing. I couldn't even hear my own bass above the chatter in the room. It was getting busy by then, very busy. And there were a hundred conversations going on, all struggling to be heard above the rest. It was clear that no one in the room could hear anything we were doing; most of them didn't even seem to notice we were there. They stood in their groups, drinking the free wine, and every now and again one of them would glance towards us and look confused. They'd frown for a few moments, watching Alistair doing his little dance, then they'd shake their heads and go back to whatever they'd been talking about before as if they'd just experienced a brief and bewildering hallucination.

After the third or fourth song, even Alistair had to admit we were wasting our time, and he agreed it was time to call it quits. We packed up our stuff and went home.

It took a few days for Alistair's enthusiasm to recover after that outing, but when the memory had started to fade, he bounced back with his ambitions for us stronger than ever and told us about the plan he'd made for our first full-length concert.

*

Raglin Street Rattle did eventually make it to The Halt Bar. Diane was very nervous and just before we climbed up onto the stage she said we weren't ready for this, but we were.

We were there to do three songs, 'Where Did You Go?', 'On Brilliant Wings' and 'Something, Something, Something', and me and David had worked to make sure we were ready even when we were at the stage of writing the songs. We'd taken all the lessons we'd

40

learned from our first two bands and fixed the things that didn't work.

I'd always found it difficult to make my vocals heard above a live drum kit too, so we pitched the vocal part higher to let it cut through, and David took to using brushes instead of sticks.

Then there was the whole experiment of me taking up the bass so's we could get the simple parts we were after, rather than having a frustrated lead guitarist soloing away underneath everything. And we'd practised long and hard to become a good rhythm section, then found a guitarist whose sound and style fitted in perfectly with what we were doing. We were ready, and despite Diane's qualms we got through all three songs without anything going wrong.

Then we went back the next Saturday with three more songs and did it all again.

Afterwards, in a letter to my friend Karn, I said: 'Although we're still a week or two away from being ready for full gigs we've played twice in The Halt Bar on Saturday afternoons at their unplugged sessions. And it was quite fine. The compère guy, he loves us. In fact he even said that into the microphone this week. "I love them…" And before we went on he came over and said, "Do you all want to go on next, 'cause we really need someone good."'

I felt like we were finally getting somewhere. It seemed that my idea to learn the bass had paid off, and I was keen to get out and start doing some full-length shows.

While we were rehearsing for the next Lisa Helps the

Blind gig, Alistair also asked me to join a country band he played in, whose bass player had just left. The band revolved around a singer called Robin who wrote songs in the style of Johnny Cash and Hank Williams, and it also featured the infamous drum machine that had caused so much friction in Lisa Helps the Blind. I'd never really been a fan of country music, but I liked Robin's songs and it was a chance to learn some new styles on the bass, so I decided to give it a go.

This was one project that moved at a pace that suited Alistair. They gave me a tape with their whole set on it, and after one rehearsal in the room with the twisted mannequins, I was suddenly out playing live with them. It was a bit of a shock to the system, but it was even more of a shock when I found out that I'd be getting paid for every show I did with them. I was suddenly making money from music for the first time in my life, after almost ten years of not making a penny. It felt kind of weird. It felt kind of weird to have somehow ended up in three bands at the same time too, but the aim had been to get as much experience on the bass as I possibly could, so I stuck with it, to hone my skills for Raglin Street Rattle.

5

Alistair's solution to the difficulties we'd faced with our first two Lisa Helps the Blind gigs was to make sure we had complete control of the environment our third one took place in. We'd got to the point where we sounded pretty good in rehearsal, but we didn't seem able to take that sound out into the world. So Alistair's plan was to bring the world, or as much of it as would fit, into rehearsals. He'd decided to set up a gig in his front room, for a small invited audience, and it seemed like it might work.

We rehearsed a set of eight songs, including 'Lord Anthony', 'Perfection As a Hipster', 'Beautiful' and 'Dear Catastrophe Waitress', and on the evening of the gig Alistair begged and borrowed twenty chairs and arranged them all in rows facing the bay window, with a little aisle down the middle.

Stuart invited two or three people. I didn't invite anyone. And Alistair invited the rest of the audience, which probably amounted to about twenty-five people. When they started to arrive I began to get nervous about how things would go. They were a bewildering assortment of hard rock and S&M fans, for the most part, and when I looked at the programme Stuart had placed on each seat, like the hymn sheets laid out on the pews before a church service, I didn't think this could go well. The front of the programme featured cartoons of hipsters drawn by Stuart, and inside there was a list of the songs we would play, along with a description of each one, and a manifesto explaining what we were about. I didn't think it had much in common with what these people were about.

We'd set up in the bay window, and gradually the audience took their seats. It was like looking out at a private memorial service for a heavy-metal god, mostly a blur of black leather and hair.

And then Stuart asked everyone to stop talking, which took them a bit by surprise, and after a quick tune-up we started to play our delicate songs, about schoolkids and disenchanted ponies.

I thought they might just get us killed.

There was a scene in *The A-Team* during the Eighties, where Boy George and Culture Club had to perform 'Karma Chameleon' for a barroom full of rednecks. Their chances of making it through the song and getting out of the bar alive didn't look good at the outset, but as George sang, the crowd suddenly started to get into it. They had a change of heart, and George emerged a hero from the terrifying ordeal.

That didn't quite happen to Lisa Helps the Blind in Alistair's living room. None of the hairy rockers began to cry, overcome by the repressed feelings they'd been head-banging away for too long. No one threw off their leathers and began to dance like a flower person. But, on the plus side, nobody pulled a knife, and everyone listened politely to what we were doing.

It was a curious sight to witness. Stuart stared straight ahead during the songs, fixing his gaze on the wall at the back of the room. Alistair did his little dance, and halfway through the shirt came off. But the most impressive thing about it all was that Stuart stood and played his songs without making any compromises, or making any allowances for the obvious differences between the audience's tastes and what we were doing. I was aware that if I'd found myself playing my own songs in front of that audience, in that setting, I wouldn't even have expected them to listen, much less take anything from it. I would certainly have been self-deprecating between songs, making it clear that I knew they didn't like what I was doing. But Stuart didn't do any of that. He just remained himself, allowing the audience and band to exist in stark contrast to each other. He presented his vision to them undiluted, and it didn't seem to matter to him whether they liked it or not. And I was slightly amazed to find you could get away with that.

Afterwards, Alistair introduced me to the guy I'd replaced as bass player in the country band. He was simply called 'The Animal'. He said that Lisa Helps the Blind wasn't his type of thing, but that we'd sounded quite good anyway. And we had. We'd played as well as we did in rehearsal, and for the first time in our short history, everyone had been able to hear us.

It felt like the beginning of something, but as it turned out, it was actually the end. Soon afterwards, I was sitting in a café near Beatbox with Alistair, and he told me that things had come to a head for him. He said he was going to give Stuart an ultimatum. Either Stuart agreed to do things at the pace Alistair thought we should be doing them, and make a proper drive for success, or else Alistair would leave.

'Stuart's songs make me feel the way songs made me feel when I was sixteen,' he said. 'I've been listening to pop music for so long I always know where a song's going to go. But Stuart's songs always go somewhere different.'

He looked off out the window, then shook his head.

'It's crunch time,' he said.

I didn't think his ultimatum was a good idea. Stuart still wasn't well enough to do any more than we were doing. But Alistair was adamant.

'I have to make it soon or not at all,' he said. 'I don't have the time to wait around.'

So he made his stand.

I wasn't there when he talked to Stuart, but I heard from both of them individually that Alistair wouldn't be working with Lisa Helps the Blind any more. It all seemed quite amicable, but now it was suddenly just Stuart and me. Alistair had brought us together, then disappeared and left us to get on with it.

With the money I'd saved up from playing bass with the country band, and the extra £10 a week I was getting for attending Beatbox, I realised I could probably afford to move to Glasgow now, if I could qualify for Housing

Benefit to pay the rent. It seemed like the ideal time to do it because Diane, the guitarist in Raglin Street Rattle, worked for one of the biggest landlords in Glasgow, doing viewings for flats all over the city. So one afternoon I got her to drive me round to look at some vacant rooms.

There were two places I liked, both on the same street as the Art School. One of them was an attic room, a bit like I had at home but bigger, and you could stand up straight in most of it. I sat in there with Diane at the end of the day and tried to decide.

'It's between this one and the one down the street,' I told her. 'Maybe I should see the other one again.'

But she couldn't find the keys for the other one. She'd lost them somewhere.

'I'll take this one, then,' I told her. 'This'll do.'

And I signed some papers.

There were eight bedrooms in the flat, four upstairs and four downstairs, plus a large kitchen and two bathrooms. At the moment, there were only two people living there: Rhonda, who was a town planner, and Michael, who had the biggest room in the flat but who never came out of it. All the other rooms were ready and waiting to be taken by students when the universities opened again. I moved my meagre belongings up a few days later and settled in. It was only a ten-minute walk to Beatbox, rather than the hour on the train I'd been travelling every day, and all at once I was living in one of Glasgow's blond sandstone tenements, where I'd always wanted to be.

It was only after Alistair left Lisa Helps the Blind that I

started getting to know Stuart properly, and we became friends. When I moved into my new place, Stuart was living in a flat on Sauchiehall Street, the street parallel to my own. And we went round to each other's places to play our new songs, discovering what we had in common.

In a letter to Karn, I wrote:

'I think you would like Stuart. He's kind of like us. He's always talking about Kerplunk, and Aqua Boy, and Parma Violet-type sweets, and *Catcher in the Rye*. And he sings songs like The Pastels and all that. And he looks like that too. So he would probably be your friend. If you knew him.'

But it was the things we didn't like that made us realise we should keep working together. Neither of us liked most of the things that seemed to be obligatory if you were in a band. We didn't like blues music or drugs, neither of us drank very much or smoked, and we were both anti-machismo. We were just making music because we loved songs—not to get rich or to get out of our heads. We'd both grown up listening to music on the same tinny Dansette record players without much bass and with plenty of crackle, and we thought that's how music should sound. We'd grown up listening to different records on those machines, and we'd come up with different solutions and visions for how to go about things in opposition to the accepted way, but we were both doing things for similar reasons, from a similar point of view.

There was one marked difference between us though. Most of the people I knew at that point who wrote songs or were in bands were fully focused on finding a record deal, myself included. That was considered to be the ultimate validation that what you were doing was worthwhile. But for Stuart, all that mattered was finding a group of people who believed in his songs enough to want to be in his band. He wanted his own band more than anything else in the world.

One of his favourite groups at that time was Tindersticks, and he often spoke of how lucky Stuart Staples (the singer and songwriter) was to have all those people wanting to play on his songs. The number seemed to matter. Having a big band like that, of the right-minded people, who were desperate to play your songs, seemed to be the only approval Stuart was interested in.

For years, he'd been putting posters up in music shops and cafés, looking for potential band mates. Sometimes his posters were cryptic, sometimes just a list of bands he liked. I don't think he'd ever had any replies—he had a clear idea of the people he'd like to find, but so far no one had come forward. Finding those people, though, had become his constant aim.

It was a concept I hadn't really come across before. Most people around Glasgow threw their bands together with whoever was closest to hand, and there were already quite a few people at Beatbox who were willing to be in Stuart's band. But he had an ideal vision in mind and he didn't want to compromise it.

Stuart's songwriting became insanely prolific around this time too. He was often writing three new songs a day, and an unreasonable percentage of them were good songs. He said that the songs often started out as jokes, and then developed into something real. That

49

seemed to perplex him, even made him sad. But he continued to think up the jokes, and the jokes continued to turn into songs and sometimes he was writing them too fast for me to learn before he'd discarded them again. I'd go to watch him doing a solo acoustic spot at The Halt Bar, or supporting other songwriters, and he'd do songs I'd never heard before and would never hear again. There was one called 'Adidas', which was simply a list of all the things Adidas had been claimed to be an acronym for when we were at school; another about jazz boys and jazz girls which made me stop in wonder. Many more. But most of them were never finished.

'I think the secret to finishing a song,' he said to me one evening, 'is knowing what the song's about before you start.'

That seemed to be a revelation for him, and his songs really started to take shape after that. He got a batch together that he decided he would record in the Beatbox studio if his day ever came around. We did some rehearsals with David Campbell on drums, to knock them into shape, and we waited. Raglin Street Rattle was waiting to get in there too. So were a lot of other people, but the sessions for the band in the posters on the Beatbox wall continued to take precedence.

One afternoon, standing outside the metal door at Beatbox, underneath the flyover that led up into the business park, Stuart asked me if I'd be the bass player in his band, if he could ever get one together. I said I'd help him put his band together, help him to get it going, but that I had my own band and my own thing to be doing.

'I'd really like you to be in my band,' he said.

'I'll help you put it together,' I repeated.

And so it seemed that we'd come to a mixed-up agreement.

6

During my first couple of weeks in the new flat, the other rooms which had been unoccupied began to fill up. First to arrive after me was a girl called Arlene, who like Rhonda had come from Northern Ireland. Arlene had come to study something vague at Caledonian College, as vague to her as it was to us, and by the end of her second month on the course she'd only spent four or five days there. On the other hand, after a week in Glasgow she'd already secured two jobs—one in the King's Café and one in The Garage nightclub, neither of which had any jobs on offer when she went looking. She was a force of nature—and her job-hunting method had involved deciding where she would like to work and then going in and convincing them they needed to employ her.

'I don't think I've ever met *anyone* like you, Arlene,' Rhonda said to her after a couple of days. 'Have you ever met anyone like her, Stuart?'

I'd never met anyone like either of them. Rhonda had the combined characteristics of being absolutely tiny, spending her weekends training with the Territorial Army and shouting 'Basil' randomly while making her dinner, in imitation of Sybil in *Fawlty Towers*.

For about a week it was just the three of us living there—along with Michael, who still never came out of his room. Then, one weekend, everyone else arrived at once.

Iain Caution came from Glenrothes to work near Charing Cross as a civil engineer. He was six foot seven, very laid-back and gentle. He was much too tall for the sloped ceilings of the attic rooms, so he took the room opposite Michael's on the ground floor. Each time he met someone new, Iain would say in his slow, easy manner,

'So, what is it you do then, mate?'

And no matter what answer they gave he would say, 'Sound,' nodding quietly. Then ask them if they wanted some beans on toast.

Richard Colburn came from Perth, giving up his career as a semi-professional snooker player to enrol on a music business course at Stow College. He took the last remaining attic room, upstairs with Arlene, Rhonda and me, and while his parents helped him to move his belongings in they quickly painted the walls and ceiling too—brilliant white. Owing to his overactive taste buds, Richard declined Iain's repeated offers of beans on toast, the sauce of the baked beans being much too strong for him. He stuck with his own dinner-time staples of plain pasta, a wheat cracker on a white-flour roll, or—occasionally—a packet of uncooked pea pods.

The tiny box room next to the kitchen was taken by a teenager called Gillian, who—much to my horror—turned out to have legged it from the same small town as I had: Alexandria. She'd moved to the city to work on the help desk at PC World, and she mostly talked about boys and getting drunk at the weekend, and sulked around in the kitchen like a normal teenager.

The eighth room in the flat, next door to Iain's room and across the hall from Gillian's, stayed mysteriously locked and unoccupied—and over the course of the next few weeks it took on a personality all of its own, as if it was another flatmate, charismatic and aloof.

This was my first experience of sharing a flat with people my own age, and the potential for adventures seemed limitless. It was a sharp change from the recent few years of isolation I'd spent living and working in my parents' attic, and in another letter to Karn, I wrote:

'We all go out a lot together. It's like the perfect accidental mix of people, and we've turned the kitchen into a living room. Anytime you feel like some company you can just go down to the kitchen and play Connect 4 or watch a film. It could just be a honeymoon period I suppose, and soon we'll turn into the most violent flat in Glasgow. But it's fun just now anyway.'

The guy who had been lying down in the posters on the Beatbox walls, stripped to his vest and propped up on one elbow, was called John McLaughlin. He didn't have any specific tutor's role on the course, unlike most of the other members of the band, but he did arrange gigs in different venues around the city, and his main involvement with the course was finding places on the bills for Beatbox bands.

I'd handed him a tape of Raglin Street Rattle just a few days after I started at Beatbox, keen to get us out playing as soon as possible. But week after week went by without him arranging anything for us. Now and again I would take a break from the computer golf and trail down the corridor to knock on the office door, seeking him out to see if there was any news. He was always friendly, trying his best to disguise the fact that he'd forgotten who I was again, and the longer it all went on the more I began to dread my trips down the corridor to look for him. I'd always hated asking people to do things for me, and having to ask them again when they hadn't delivered on their promise was torture. But the thought of getting nowhere with my band was torture too. The conflicting impulses of wanting to avoid pressing John to find us a gig fought constantly with the desire to get somewhere, and about once a week I'd muster all my resolve and have another crack at it.

It was quite clear to me that he didn't like my tape, but finally I wore him down and he put us on the bill of an all-day festival at a club on the corner of George Square called The Brewhouse. Diane, of course, insisted that we weren't ready to play a full set in public, but we stepped up the rehearsal schedule and worked on seven or eight songs. They included 'Where Did You Go?', 'On Brilliant Wings', 'She Called My Name', 'Everything That Shines' and 'Something, Something, Something', all collaborations written with David, and by the day of the festival they were sounding good.

We were scheduled to play in the middle of the

afternoon, and it turned out to be a stiflingly hot day. Not the sort of afternoon anyone would want to waste in a dark and airless club when the sun shone so rarely in Glasgow. The arrangement had been that the drum kit and the amplifiers would be provided by the organisers of the event; all we had to bring were our guitars and a set of drumsticks. So we turned up to play our set, only to find that there was no drum kit and no amplifiers at all, just a PA system and a couple of microphones. The guy who was meant to be bringing the rest of the stuff had seemingly decided it was too nice a day for him to be inside too, and things had been rearranged to turn the event into an acoustic festival.

We had a meeting to decide whether we should pull out. Eventually Diane decided we should go through with it because it might be the last chance we got to do a show together.

'How come?' David asked her, and she told us she'd finalised plans to go and live in Australia for six months, just a few days earlier.

'But I can't play,' David said. 'There aren't any drums.'

So in the end Diane borrowed an acoustic guitar from one of the other bands and we did it just the two of us, sitting on high bar stools, while David joined the sparse audience to watch the final public appearance of Raglin Street Rattle. I enjoyed the freedom of singing without having to play bass, and it was good to be able to play a full set of songs for once. Stuart turned up to watch just before we were due to go on. He sat with David near the door, where they could still see the sunshine outside, and he wore a pair of yellow earplugs while we played. Given the low volume of our set, it wasn't likely that he heard anything at all.

With Diane's surprise announcement that she was leaving to spend time in Australia, I didn't have the heart to go through the whole process of finding a guitarist again. David and I kept our fingers crossed that our day in the Beatbox studio would arrive before Diane left, and David started planning another one of his regular American road trips for the near future. I'd hoped the tape we recorded at Beatbox would be our calling card, something we could send out to introduce the band to the world and start things happening. Instead it was going to be more like a souvenir of our marathon of rehearsals, and a document of a band that no longer existed. And that was only if our day in the studio came around in time—which wasn't a great bet, given the chaotic nature of the Beatbox diary.

It wasn't just the case that days in the studio were frequently cancelled; the opposite quite often happened too. Regularly, there would be a sudden demand that a few empty hours of studio time be filled by someone on the course when a commercial session had ended ahead of schedule, or when the government quota for course time hadn't been met by course musicians that week. It didn't matter if no one around had anything prepared or didn't have their band available at the time—the hours needed to be filled, and someone had to volunteer to fill them.

We'd already recorded one of Stuart's songs under those conditions before either of us got our properly scheduled day in the studio. Sitting around, doing nothing much, we'd been berated for our laziness and lack of motivation by the course leaders—en masse—then given an afternoon to come up with a recording to prove our dedication.

The song we recorded was called 'Pocket Book Angels', something Stuart had written a few days earlier while he was busking on Ashton Lane. It was all about busking on Ashton Lane. Almost everyone who was around that day played something on it. I played bass, Gerry Campbell the songwriting tutor played drums. 'London', a Pink Floyd addict with a flat cap, played lead guitar, soloing wherever he could find the tiniest gap to fill. It was a great pop song, probably all but beaten to death by having instrument after instrument overdubbed on it to meet our brief of filling up the afternoon, but Stuart just let the arrangement develop out of the loose parts everyone played. He didn't have any overall vision for how he wanted the recording to turn out, and it was a haphazard collaboration.

One evening, I let my dad hear the finished recording, and he said, 'You should stick with that band. I like that. They'll go places.'

'It's not really a band,' I told him. 'It was just a one-off thing.'

'They'll go far,' he said. 'Stick with them.'

After all the cancellations and reschedulings, the false starts and the near misses, both me and Stuart did eventually get our days in the Beatbox studio. David hadn't left for his American trip before Stuart's day came around, so he was there to play drums, and Diane was still in the country for mine. Both sessions were only a few days apart, but in character they were quite different.

With Raglin Street Rattle, the songs were so well rehearsed and we knew our parts so well that it was just a case of making a record of how the band sounded. Diane overdubbed a second guitar part on each of the three songs we recorded, but apart from that the instrumental tracks were live takes, which I added the vocals to afterwards. We recorded 'Where Did You Go?', 'On Brilliant Wings' and 'Something, Something, Something', all mainly acoustic, spare and untreated.

Although Alistair was no longer on the course at Beatbox, he came back to watch me record, and sat with Stuart on the sofa in the control room. He hadn't seen Raglin Street Rattle before, though he knew all the songs we were recording, and when I came back through from the live room he said, 'I didn't know you could sing with feeling. I'm surprised.'

Steve MacKenzie was engineering the session. Steve was a fellow inmate on the course who'd managed to get himself an education in using the studio by helping out on commercial sessions. These always took place behind locked doors, but Steve had somehow managed to gain entry, and—as inexperienced as he was—he was soon single-handedly engineering all the non-commercial studio sessions. The course leaders didn't seem to mind that he still didn't know how everything worked, or that the sheer scale of the workload left him constantly exhausted. Maybe they thought there was no point in wasting a more qualified engineer on the inmates' demos, so the sessions all fell to Steve, without even a tape op to help him out.

People were always asking Steve to do things that were at the limits of his knowledge, and during the Raglin Street Rattle session two instruments ended up on the same track—a guitar and a snare drum, I think. David wasn't happy about it, but Steve found a way to make it work, and we came out with a good record of what the band had sounded like.

It was a successful realisation of the vision David and I had set out with even before I'd had my brainwave to learn the bass, back when we'd started writing the songs together. It seemed to me to have the potential to go further, but that was as far as it went.

Steve engineered Stuart's day in the studio too, and we recorded four songs—'Dog on Wheels', 'String Bean Jean', 'The State I'm In', and 'Belle and Sebastian'. It was a very different kind of session from my own, with Stuart building up arrangements track by track, making full use of the other musicians on the course, bringing them in one at a time to overdub their parts and then disappear again.

Although the set-up was similar to when we'd been ushered into the studio to record 'Pocket Book Angels', Stuart's attitude was different this time. The arrangement of 'Pocket Book Angels' had emerged out of a combination of improvisation and collaboration, but for these recordings, Stuart was firmly in charge, with a clear vision of exactly how he wanted the sounds and the arrangement to be. We'd only rehearsed the rhythm section beforehand, just the three of us—David, Stuart and me—so it wasn't like the Raglin Street Rattle session where we were making a document of something we'd already been playing. It was a case of creating the record in the studio, with Stuart's ideas struggling against what was possible with the available equipment, and it continually pushed Steve's knowledge to the limits.

The unconventional approach Stuart took to the recordings began right at the start, when he decided to lay down his acoustic guitar parts on tape first, along with a scratch vocal, and work upwards from there. There were no click tracks, no percussion instruments, and the tempo of his guitar wandered around unconstrained, following the wonky metronome in his head. When David turned up at the studio, that part of the session was already complete, and David had to play the drums in time with the guitar, taking the strumming as his guide, speeding up and slowing down in little increments as he went.

Steve was baffled by the approach initially, and he struggled gamely to reorganise the set-up to try and make it work, going against all the rudimentary techniques and procedures he'd learned so far. David wasn't too keen on the situation either. As far as he was concerned, the drummer sets the timing; everyone else follows the beat the drummer is keeping. But Stuart's conviction was that his own vocal performance of the song should set the pace, and that it should be a fluid thing. It's a common approach in folk music, particularly in unaccompanied ballad singing, but it met with some resistance amongst musicians used to playing pop and rock, where the beat holds primary importance.

David soon got some good takes on the songs,

though, with Steve doing everything he could to make the acoustic guitar loud enough in David's headphones to be heard above his own playing. I added my bass once the drums were down, just playing in the control room with my bass plugged directly into the desk. I didn't have my own amp yet, and usually just played through a practice amp Stuart had lent me. The main advantage of playing in the control room, though, was it meant my fingers didn't seize up from the freezing cold in the live room. David had come back through almost blue, and for a while we thought we might need to send out for a tin-foil blanket to get his core temperature back up to human again.

Besides using the musicians on the course, Stuart also brought in a few people from the outside world to play more unusual instruments. Mick Cooke came in and quickly played the trumpet part on 'Dog on Wheels', Brian Nugent played flute on 'Belle and Sebastian' and Beatbox tutor Gerry played the surf guitar riff on 'String Bean Jean' and keyboards on 'The State I Am In' and 'Belle and Sebastian'.

Stuart had two distinct ways of using the musicians at his disposal. If they were to play a melody line, he'd usually written their part for them beforehand, and he'd tell them exactly what to play. But for the more general accompaniment parts he'd know what instrument he wanted to be there, and he'd know what he didn't want it to sound like, but he left the musician to make up their own part and then guided them towards the way he wanted it to be. That was the way Gerry's keyboard parts evolved on 'The State I Am In' and 'Belle and Sebastian'. Gerry had a strong idea of what he could add to those songs, and Stuart encouraged him go with it, even letting him add his own intro piece to 'Belle and Sebastian'.

My favourite song of the session was 'String Bean Jean'. I loved the vocal melody, I loved the guitar riff and I loved the chord sequence. But more than anything I loved the way Stuart had managed to illuminate his everyday life in the lyrics, with everyday language, and make it all seem quite magical by floating it up above everything on a pretty tune. 'Rock School' or 'The School of Rock' was how Stuart usually referred to Beatbox, and the conversational way he drops that into the lyrics and then goes on to talk about hanging around waiting for his flatmates to finish work was a level of ordinariness I hadn't heard in a pop song before. I'd come across it in poetry, but even the most determinedly realistic pop lyricists, like Morrissey or Jarvis Cocker, still used relatively heightened language—still explored an emotional landscape in their songs—still reached towards elsewhere and escape, still invoked a sense of longing for an alternative life. 'String Bean Jean' just lit up an ordinary day, in ordinary language, with a tale of ordinary people doing ordinary things, dispensing with even the brief moment of epiphany that most realist writers rely upon.

There was a point during the session when we took a break, to get something to eat and to give Steve some time to break down the set-up and assemble a new one for something else Stuart wanted to try. Just as we were leaving the studio, I noticed Steve looked exhausted.

'Are you doing OK?' I asked him.

He nodded.

It hadn't been easy-going for him. At every stage, his normal way of working had been interrupted and renegotiated. His regular practice had been deemed unsuitable, and he'd had to reset the parameters of his outboard equipment and patch things together in ways he hadn't done before, trying to meet Stuart's expectations for the way things should sound without really knowing the equipment well enough to use it in any way other than how he'd been taught.

It was clear that if we'd had Kris or Happy engineering, they would have imposed their own singular mode of operation on the session; there wouldn't have been any room for manoeuvre. They were too experienced and too convinced that the way they made things sound, with their compressors and drum mics and reverbs, was the way things should sound. The way things sounded on the radio, and in clubs—tight and clean and punchy, smooth and shining. Steve was enough of a beginner that he didn't yet have his habits set in stone, and he was still willing to find out through experimentation if things could be different. But, even so, I'd watched him biting his tongue and fighting against his frustration at various points throughout the day—and it looked like it was beginning to get to him.

I stayed behind for a while after everyone else had left to offer him some moral support, and to make sure the tensions didn't stop the session before we got to the end, but I didn't really need to bother.

'Stuart just knows what he wants,' Steve said resignedly, and not without a note of admiration in his voice. I'd had the feeling that Stuart's lack of compromise and quick dismissal of Steve's ideas would have alienated him, made him unwilling to continue working with Stuart; it's certainly what I would have expected to happen in my own session if I'd been so blunt—but I was wrong. Although there had been tension and conflict, it had only increased Steve's respect for what Stuart was trying to do. He got to work on reassembling the set-up, while I left him to it and went for my break.

A couple of years later, after we'd made two albums, the songs from that session were released as the Belle and Sebastian EP 'Dog on Wheels'. They were released exactly as Steve recorded them, unaltered, proving that although he was still finding his way as an engineer, in a very limited studio, he'd managed to realise Stuart's vision for the songs. Stressed as he was, and pushed to his limit, he'd done a great job.

The rest of the afternoon continued with a few more overdubs and Stuart adding some vocal harmonies, and then the mixing began. It was a labour-intensive affair; the desk had no automation, and all the changes had to be done in real time, Stuart and Steve performing the final mixes between them, standing side by side at the desk, while the results bounced down from videotape onto DAT. And when it was done, although we didn't know it at the time, we had made the first 'Belle and Sebastian' record. Stuart had made the first recording of any of his songs that he felt measured up to the way they sounded in his head.

7

By the time we'd both finished our sessions in the Beatbox studio, I was beginning to get used to life in the flat with my crazy new family of seven. There was rarely a quiet moment—mainly due to Arlene and Rhonda, who had become an incorrigible double act, always in at everything.

Rhonda, it turned out, was something of an exhibitionist. When she wasn't planning towns, or off training with the Territorial Army, her next favourite thing to do was undress in the kitchen. That, and Arlene's ability to turn any stranger she met into a virtual member of her family within fifteen minutes of meeting them, meant that the kitchen was quite often full of boys we didn't know—half of them there in the hope that Rhonda would perform the trick they'd heard so much about, and the other half having mistaken Arlene's affability for something else altogether and fallen in love with her.

Richard would sit amongst the chaos eating his pea

pods and smiling calmly like a wise Buddha, occasionally giving in to Rhonda's requests for him to stroke her earlobe to help her relax. Gillian, still a teenager, would talk excitedly, unable for the most part to draw any of the boys' attention away from Rhonda and Arlene, and Iain would lazily ask one of the boys what they did for a living, and then tell them what they did was sound and offer to make them beans on toast.

The most charismatic character in the flat, though—and the one we all remained most intrigued by—was the eighth, unoccupied room; the one whose door remained firmly locked.

At first we'd assumed there was someone still to arrive; that any day now a new flatmate would appear and introduce themselves, and the mystery would be over. But it didn't happen. No one came. No one even enquired about the room.

We considered, after a few weeks, getting the money together to rent it between us. We thought we could move the TV from the kitchen in there and have a communal place to hang out, away from the clatter of dishes and the smell of cooking. But none of us could afford even a seventh share of the rent, and we fell instead to occasionally making half-hearted attempts at picking the lock, which always failed.

Then one night, Iain had a brainwave.

There were only the two of us at home, sitting in the kitchen on the plastic chairs, watching a sitcom on TV after dinner, getting more and more uncomfortable as the evening wore on.

'If we had that other room,' Iain said, 'we could put a sofa in there. And a couple of armchairs. Imagine it.'

So, bored by the show, we went out into the hall and studied the door again. We leant against it heavily and thought about unscrewing the fixings round the handle, and then Iain's idea struck him.

'I know how to get in,' he said, and dragged me into the bathroom next door to the eighth room, then strode to the window on the back wall.

'There's another window like this one in the room next door, right?' he said, and I nodded. This window was tall, in two parts, the bottom part sliding up over the top when it was open.

'So all I have to do,' he said, 'is open this window, climb out and along to the windowsill of the room next door, open that window, and then we're in. Simple. Help me get this one open.'

Straight away it was clear that there were flaws in his plan. Most obviously, the window in the room next door was probably locked from the inside, so there would be no way of getting it open from out there. Then there was the fact that even if he did get into the room the door would still be locked. It was secured with a mortice lock, which needed a key, not just with a latch on the other side of the door. Anyone else who wanted to join him in there would have to go out and in through the window too, along with any sofas or TVs he wanted in there. More important than any of these relatively minor points, though, was the fact that we were up on the fourth storey of the building, with a fifty-foot drop down into the garden below—about ten feet separating the windowsill of the bathroom from the windowsill of the eighth room. There were only about six inches of sill jutting out from the window, and it was

68

pitch dark outside.

'I'm going for it,' Iain said. 'I have to get in there.'

There was one more drawback to his plan, though. The bathroom window was jammed shut. He'd unfastened the latch halfway up, where the two frames met, and he was tugging at the rings on the bottom frame, trying to haul it up—but he'd only managed to open the window by about an inch and a half and it wasn't going any further.

'Give me a hand,' he said, and I told him he should probably leave it alone, think up something else. 'Nonsense,' he said, 'it's just jammed up with paint. Grab a hold of that handle.'

He was thoroughly consumed by the elegance of his idea, so I took hold of the hoops and gave it enough of a tug to know it wasn't going anywhere. While I did that, Iain banged the frame with his palms and tried to dislodge it.

'Keep pulling,' he said, and he pushed at the glass, all sense of reason gone. It seemed to me that if we did get the window open he was so fired up he wouldn't think twice before stepping out onto the windowsill and then swiftly plunging into the garden below.

'Forget it,' I said, 'it's a crazy idea.'

'Keep pulling,' he replied. 'I think it's moving.'

He banged the side of his fist against the glass, shaking it backwards and forwards, and then good luck intervened. The bottom pane he was pushing against smashed and his hand went through it, the glass cutting his hand as it fell and suddenly bringing him back to the realm of sense and reason.

'Bastard!' he shouted, then he pushed his hand over

69

the sink and turned the tap on. Mixing with the water, the amount of blood running down the plughole looked substantial, and we decided to go to the hospital to get it stitched. I handed him a towel, which he wrapped tightly around the cut, and we went down into the street to look for a taxi, since the phone only took incoming calls.

'I probably got a bit carried away there,' Iain said, as we sat in the back seat of the cab, trundling along Sauchiehall Street, watching the towel turning red. He was more or less back to his slowly nodding self now, grinning knowingly at his earlier loss of sanity. 'Just as well I didn't get the window open,' he said. 'I'd have killed myself.'

'Definitely,' I said, and he eased the towel away to take a look at his hand.

By the time we reached the hospital and climbed out of the taxi the bleeding had stopped. He thought about going inside to find out if it needed stitches or anything, but in the end he decided not to bother.

'I'll put a plaster on it at home,' he said. 'It'll be fine.'

So we went looking for another taxi to take us back to the flat again, and set about trying to think up a story to tell the landlord in the morning, to explain the broken bathroom window.

*

Work with the country band was always regular. We played mainly in pubs, sometimes doing our whole set twice with an interval in between. Alistair kept telling Robin he needed to write new songs, to give us a longer set-list, and Robin brought a new song along to rehearsals most weeks—but by the time we'd learned it and rehearsed it he would have grown tired of an older one and wanted to drop that—so the number of songs stayed more or less constant.

As time went on, I started to feel uncomfortable about being in a country band. I'd got a lot better on bass, playing with them. Having to play long sets, with the big grey drum machine and its rigid pulse, had strengthened my fingers and improved my timing—but the country bass lines were getting overly familiar: the root note and the fifth of the three major chords, with the order rarely altered from one song to the next. It had become a job, and a job was the one thing I'd promised myself I'd always avoid. The relationship between Alistair and Robin was becoming fraught too. Alistair often berated Robin for his erratic performances, telling him he had to get more professional, that he had to start taking things seriously.

One night, after we played a double set in the Clutha Vaults, a couple of Alistair's friends came and talked to us while we were packing up our gear. They were different from his usual friends: less hairy, devoid of leather, more hip. I think they were going out together, and after a while the girl said to me,

'You don't look as if you should be in this band.'

'Why not?' I asked, but she just shrugged.

'She's right,' the boy said.

'You should be doing something else,' the girl said, and I zipped my bass into its bag.

It seemed like a strange conversation, but it got me thinking. It was what I was already feeling.

71

We had one more gig lined up, a competition on a Saturday afternoon in a new venue in Paisley. Alistair had high hopes for it—he thought we could take a big cash prize. And he thought it would further the band's career, if we practised enough. To me, an afternoon talent show in Paisley was almost reason enough to get out of the band there and then, but I decided to go through with it, and deal with leaving when it was out of the way.

I let slip to a couple of friends I usually saw on Saturday afternoons that I was playing the gig, mainly to explain why I couldn't see them that weekend. To my dismay, though, they were both waiting at the venue when we arrived, there to lend their support. No one I knew had seen me perform with the country band before, and I realised I didn't feel comfortable about it. It was something I wanted to do anonymously. I didn't want it to be a part of my identity in any way. On the other hand, if it hadn't been for my friends, the cavernous venue would have been almost empty when we climbed onstage. A few other acts sat around the edges of the room, mainly facing away from the stage, and there was a barman and the guy who was running the show, but that was the full extent of the audience.

'Just stay focused,' Alistair told us as we plugged our guitars in and he switched on the drum machine. 'We can win this. We can do it. Forget about the audience, just do what we've been doing in rehearsals. It's ours for the taking.'

But we didn't play well. Or more accurately, Robin didn't play well. He forgot words, played wrong chords, fell out of step with the drum machine. I looked out at my two friends sitting facing us on high bar stools in the middle of the room, their pint glasses sitting in front of them on a high suspended table that ran out from the bar. They smiled encouragingly while Alistair glared angrily at the back of Robin's head, giving him a verbal dressing down between songs, apologising over the microphone while Robin tuned up. He seemed to be taking Robin's mistakes personally, and tried to make up for them by dancing even more enthusiastically than usual and singing his backing vocals with all the passion he could muster, while the booming drum machine reverberated like a machine-gun attack in the empty room.

Eventually the whole sorry episode ended with Alistair refusing to talk to Robin when we came off stage, and I went out to sample the delights of Paisley with my friends and planned my phone call to Alistair to tell him I was leaving.

When I was nine or ten, I suddenly got tired of going to The Boys' Brigade and decided I wanted out. It had started to seem stupid to me, all the drilling and the uniforms and the organised games in the cold church hall, and I wanted more time at home to watch TV and read my comics. I couldn't find the courage to tell the leaders I wanted to leave, though, and I just kept going, week after week, continually hoping I'd find the nerve to make each meeting my last, then telling myself it would all be easier to do next week—all the way from summer to Christmas.

The same thing happened a couple of years later when I wanted to leave the football team to have more time for fishing. It took me forever to do it. After that, I made a decision to stop joining things. It was just too much work when I wanted out again. But now I'd joined the country band, and I didn't find it any easier than before, preparing to make my exit. I spent the morning after the Paisley show gearing up to it, backing out of it and talking myself back into it again. Then, after lunch, I dialled Alistair's number and waited to see what would happen.

'That was a horrible gig,' Alistair said. 'Horrible.' And he started outlining his plans for how we should do things in the future, what we needed to fix, what we needed to work on.

'I don't want to do it any more,' I heard myself saying. I wasn't even sure if he'd heard me, I'd said it so quickly.

There was a pause, a sigh, and then Alistair said, 'I'm not surprised. Not after the way Robin's been performing recently.' And as he went on to catalogue Robin's unprofessional behaviours, I decided that was as good a reason as any for him to think I was leaving.

'Don't worry about it,' he said. 'I understand. I'm not sure how much longer I'll put up with it myself.'

And although we still saw each other now and again, the Paisley talent show was the last time I played with Alistair. A few months later, as I walked up the steep hill to the Art School on my way home one night, I thought I saw Robin ahead of me, zigzagging drunkenly from one side of the pavement to the other. As I negotiated my way past him I got ready to say hello, but before I could he banged into me, quite powerfully, then walked on. I assumed he hadn't taken my leaving quite as amicably as Alistair had.

*

With the demise of Raglin Street Rattle, and with David off in America again, I decided to stop working on my own songs for a while. I had just published my first short story in a HarperCollins anthology, and I had brought the second draft of my third novel with me when I moved into the flat. Neither of my first two novels had been published, but with the success of my short story, I thought things were starting to look up— and I decided to concentrate on finishing the third draft of my novel when I wasn't playing bass.

I lent Stuart my copy of the HarperCollins book and he said the last sentence of my story was the best last sentence he'd read. He'd never said anything much about my songs, but he always seemed impressed that I was writing a novel. Sometimes he introduced me to people by saying, 'This is Stuart. He's writing a book.'

He often said that even when I still had my band, and something about it, coupled with the failure of the band to get anywhere, had started to make me lose confidence in my songs.

There were people around who liked what I was doing; there was the guitarist in Beatbox called London that we played with occasionally. He kept telling me he loved my songs, and that I should form a band with him to play them. And one night in the flat, when Rhonda asked Stuart and me exactly what kind of music we made, we each played a song in the kitchen for her on Stuart's acoustic guitar, and she said she preferred my kind of music. Then there was Sandy, the compère at the Halt Bar, who had always been encouraging. But nothing could help me shake the feeling that there was something about my songs I wanted to change.

Stuart's songs, along with some tunes by another Beatbox regular called Biff Smith, were really getting me interested in vocal melody, over and above everything else. Up until that point, my songwriting focus had mainly been harmonic. And as a listener, too, it was the combination of harmony and lyrics that had always interested me. But Stuart and Biff's vocal melodies were so strong, and so flagrantly dismissive of the anti-melody ideology that was permeating things at the time, that I fell under their spell. Their songs made me want to learn how to write those kinds of melodies too. So, one afternoon, I asked Stuart if he could help me out.

'We could use the piano rooms in the Mitchell Library,' I said, but he wasn't sure.

'I don't know what I could show you,' he said. 'It's not something I could teach.'

But I managed to persuade him to at least give it a shot and, in the meantime, whenever the flat was halfway quiet, I set about tidying up the third draft of my book.

Not that the flat was even halfway quiet most of the time. And that was when there were only seven of us. One evening I came home from Beatbox to find a quiet, skinny guy I'd never met before sitting alone at the kitchen table. His name was Eric, and after a few polite words he told me was waiting for Arlene to come back from college.

It felt like a familiar situation. There were always lost boys turning up at the flat looking for Arlene, while she hid in her room and asked us to shoo them away. So I told Eric she wouldn't be back for ages, and that he should probably go away and come back another time. But he just said quietly that he would wait. His assuredness was a bit disconcerting. I didn't even know how he'd got in, but I was certain he was wasting his time—and we'd have to chase him away as soon as Arlene got home. Still, he seemed determined. So I took advantage of the flat being otherwise empty and went upstairs to work on my book, leaving him to it.

One by one, the rest of the flatmates came home and found him still sitting there, quiet and composed. It was only when I went down to put something together for my dinner, and Eric briefly left the room to go to the toilet, that Rhonda filled us in on what was happening.

'That's Arlene's man,' she said, softly but quickly. 'He's come to Glasgow to study accounting. Arlene only signed up for her course so she'd already be here when he arrived.'

It turned out Arlene had picked her course more or less at random, indiscriminately enrolling on the first one that would have her, to stop her parents objecting to her following Eric from Ireland to Glasgow and staying there while he did his course.

A few minutes after Eric came back into the kitchen, Arlene arrived home and her actions confirmed what Rhonda had already told us. She started rubbing Eric's hair, bubbling with excitement and introducing him to everyone as 'my wee Eric', despite the fact that he was over six feet tall.

'Isn't he the cutest thing you've ever seen?' Arlene asked. 'Isn't he though? Look at him. He's adorable.'

She pulled at his face and played with his hair as if he was a toy, and Eric sat calm and unfazed, letting it all happen, looking at us as if to say, 'What can you do?'

It turned out that Eric had moved into another place owned by our landlord, further up the street, right next door to the Art School. Later in the evening we went up there for a while, and instead of seven occupants this place had seventeen. They all shared a canteen-like kitchen in the basement, where there were no windows, three ovens and a pool table. And so it seemed that our circle of friends, and the potential for chaotic adventure, had just increased dramatically.

PART TWO

Rhode Island

8

As Stuart's strength began to return and his health improved, he became ever more focused on finding his band. He already had a name; he'd been taking the tape we made at Beatbox to local radio stations and magazines and he'd attributed it to 'Rhode Island'. The show for new music on Radio Scotland, Beat Patrol, had already played 'Dog on Wheels', so although Rhode Island didn't exist outside Stuart's imagination yet, they'd been getting some airplay.

The first musician Stuart found to start making the band a reality was the drummer. Gary Thom, who played in the Halt Bar sessions backing up The Usual Suspects, and who until recently had been the drummer in The Moondials, told Stuart after an open mic spot that he'd love to be in his band. He was exactly the kind of drummer Stuart was looking for, so one night we rehearsed a few songs in my flat, and then walked across the city to give Gary an audition.

We were both nervous. We'd never given anyone an

audition for Stuart's band before, and we weren't sure what we would do. Just play the songs while Gary hit the drums, unable to hear us? We always played quietly, but as it turned out we needn't have worried. When we got to Gary's flat, a few minutes before the arranged time, he wasn't there. No one was. The windows were dark and the buzzer went unanswered. We hung around in the cold for almost half an hour, in case he was just late getting back from somewhere, and we pushed the buzzer every few minutes and then tried some of the others in case we'd got the wrong number, but it was clear he wasn't there. We waited until we couldn't bear the cold any longer and then decided he'd failed the audition by default, and started the long walk back across the city again.

Stuart was pretty dejected to begin with. He took Gary's absence as a comment on the quality of his songs, initially. Then, as we walked, he decided it was Gary's loss.

'People would give their right arm to play on songs as good as this,' he said. I wondered if it would still be possible to play on them once your right arm was gone. Maybe a tambourine. Maybe a Moog.

'Who can't get it together enough to turn up at their own house?' I said.

We decided that was as disorganised as it was possible to be.

From the first time I'd heard Stuart's songs, I'd always been struck by the type of characters who populated them. I'd sometimes seen those types of character around the west end, in ones and twos, dressed in charity shop clothes and National Health glasses with fake lenses, but I'd never seen them all gathered together en masse until I helped Stuart put on a night at The 13th Note on Glassford Street. An event he called The Hipster Café Tradefair.

Frustrated at still not having a band of his own to arrange a gig for, Stuart decided we should each choose a band and promote an event around them. The Hipster Café Tradefair was the result. I chose The Pop Rockets, whose singer and songwriter, Biff Smith, was a fellow inmate at Beatbox. Stuart chose Toaster, who there was already a buzz about, and who seemed to be going places. We went down to The 13th Note on Glassford Street one afternoon, and Stuart convinced the promoter Alex Huntley to let us have the venue for an evening, then he set about making plans and putting up posters.

In some ways, it was like the gig we'd done in Alistair's living room, but on a larger scale. There were programmes to be handed out at the door with a cartoon logo of hipsters at a trade fair that Stuart had designed. The same logo appeared on all the posters and flyers for the event. And the main feature of the evening was that you had to bring an object of desire to gain entry, which you then traded for an item someone else had brought and left on a table at the door. For a while, it was my job to stand behind the table, coordinating the swaps, keeping tabs on the Viewmasters and Seventies annuals, the Polaroid cameras and the obscure LPs. Someone even brought a lava lamp, and I could tell that—in contrast to the gig in Alistair's living room, when we'd played for the metalheads—this was an audience in tune with Stuart's vision.

The Pop Rockets captivated me. Biff Smith was the only unsigned songwriter I knew whose melodies were as strong as Stuart's. His voice was similar to Green Gartside's, from Scritti Politti, but his band were punky and energetic. They played a song called 'Carousel' that was breathtakingly perfect.

Toaster headlined. They played straight-ahead proto-Britpop. There was a lot of dancing onstage and it all seemed dangerously close to bandwagon jumping from where I was standing, but the audience went crazy for them. And the audience were really who the evening was about. These characters from Stuart's songs.

They fascinated me. I couldn't quite work them out. Most of them didn't seem to know each other, and yet they'd all turned up here in the same place, at the same time, dressed in a similar way to each other, all dressed like the one awkward kid in the class at school. The kid who had often been me. They were willowy creatures, both the boys and the girls, and although they looked like outsiders they all fitted in. Here.

I wondered where they'd all come from and how they knew what they knew. There was no one like that at Beatbox, no one in The Halt Bar. No one who lived in my flat dressed like that, and no one who ever came to visit looked like that either. I hadn't even come across anyone like that up at the big house next door to the Art School where Wee Eric lived.

But Stuart had called out to them, and they'd all responded to his call. They hadn't come along to listen to his own songs, they hadn't come along to see Rhode

Island, but they'd come. And it was clear that when Stuart did have his band, they were the people he wanted to come back again. From whatever corners and cafés and bedsits they usually occupied. He even had his own pet name for them. He called them the 'Bowlies'.

Meanwhile, things at Beatbox continued to get stranger and stranger. Over the course of a single weekend all the tutors but one suddenly disappeared, and the posters of the band they had been a part of were taken down from the walls. At the same time, the number of inmates on the course started to increase dramatically, and continued to increase on a daily basis. The place came to resemble an air-raid shelter during the Blitz, with as many bodies packed in as the rooms would hold. And since the studio control room was locked even more frequently than before, and the only tuition remaining was the Cubase class run by a guy called Neil Cameron, a new inmate called Kirk set up as a barber in the main corridor, putting his skills from an earlier career to use. When the computer golf began to get boring you could always go out there for a haircut.

The course leaders didn't seem to mind. We only ever saw them now during their frequent sprints up the corridor and into the control room, passing by at an alarming rate, as if something had caught fire in there. To add to the surreal atmosphere of the whole thing, Eighties pop star Alan Rankine, from The Associates, had begun to take part in these sprinting sessions too, and a few inmates would improvise a version of the riff from 'Party Fears Two' as he streaked past.

I knew from my flatmate Richard that Alan Rankine taught on the music business course at Stow College, but his appearances at Beatbox were something new, and seemed to be connected to the secret activity taking place in the studio.

By then, most people on the course were aware of the deal that had brought Beatbox into being; the organisers had wanted to set up their own studio to record and promote the bands they managed, and they'd been given government funding to do it on the condition that they also ran a course for unemployed musicians on the premises. They also received about £40 a week for every unemployed musician they took in, plus funding for tutors.

Now that the band had imploded, though, in frustration and minor violence—leaving a few broken doors and smashed ashtrays around the building—the only source of funding for the leaders' new plans was the inmates' allowances. We guessed that was why so many of us were being packed into the place: to cover what they'd lost in tutors' fees, and to fund whatever clandestine project was taking place in the studio. It certainly seemed to be something that required a lot of capital, and we came to the conclusion they were probably building a spaceship in there, to carry them away to another planet more suited to their stellar ambitions.

With the studio no longer available to us, and virtually no lessons taking place, we took to playing Stuart's songs with London to pass the time. London's real name was Mark. He'd played guitar on Stuart's Beatbox session, and he fronted a prog-improv band called Roach. We went to see them once or twice, and it was something like a nightmare to me—ten-minute versions of Pink Floyd and Led Zeppelin songs, with the false endings that recurred over and over and made me wish music had never been invented. But London had a quirky stage presence. He was the singer and lead guitarist, and he adopted a cheeky-chappy persona up there that took the edge off the horror of the whole thing. He was a great guitarist, and the rest of the band were great musicians too. They had quite a loyal following, and they were playing in good-sized venues—but for some reason London wanted to play with us, so we passed some time in Beatbox with him.

There were so many bodies in the building by then that it was hard to find a space to sit down and practise a lot of the time. We ended up taking to the freezing-cold live room of the studio and practising in there, with our guitars going out of tune halfway through every song because of the sub-zero temperatures. On quieter days we practised in the corridor, and sometimes Alan Rankine or Gordon Rintoul, the head of the course, would sprint past us with a patronising 'Keep it up, boys. Sounding great,' while they rushed on towards sculpting the future.

Stuart had continued taking his tape round the city. He'd dropped it in at *The List* magazine for a review, but they'd ignored him. Beat Patrol had played it again, and he'd been dropping it off at various venues, trying to get gigs. One afternoon he told me and London he'd been offered a gig downstairs at The 13th Note supporting The Juney Rubens, and he wanted us to play it with him. London was only half keen; there weren't enough guitar solos in Stuart's songs for his liking, but in the end he agreed. Rhode Island were ready for their first public appearance.

*

I don't know why it took me so long to find out that my flatmate Richard played drums. During weekdays, it was always just the two of us at breakfast. The same in the evenings too; we usually ate dinner together waiting for the rest of them to come home. In contrast to us, they all left very early in the morning and came back quite late at night; we were on music courses, and the hours were more relaxed than they were in the real world.

So I knew Richard had practised with some of the top snooker players back in Perth before he'd come to study at Stow, and I knew that the students on his course had to release a single by a band they chose as part of their coursework. We'd had an announcement about that at Beatbox, and I was planning to submit my Raglin Street Rattle tape when the time came. I'd asked Richard to keep me up to date with when they were ready for submissions. But I didn't know he was a musician, only that he spent a lot of time in his room listening to the widest range of music I'd ever heard.

Then one morning, while we were sitting at the kitchen table, Richard said, 'You've got something to do with Rhode Island, haven't you? Are you in that band?'

I told him it wasn't really a band yet—it was just

Stuart, with me helping him out.

He asked if I could get him a tape. One of the students on his course had heard Stuart's songs being played on Beat Patrol, and he'd liked the sound of them. The name had come up in class as a possibility for the single they were to release, and Richard recognised it from conversations we'd had. I told him I'd get him a tape, and reminded him I'd hand in one of Raglin Street Rattle too. That was when he told me he played drums.

'I'll play with you both sometime if you're looking for a drummer,' he said.

So I told Stuart there was some interest in his music already at the Stow College course, and that Richard had asked for a tape. And the next time we went to do an open mic spot at The Halt, Richard came with us.

When we'd been rehearsing with David Campbell on drums, Stuart had always tried to get David to play quieter, getting him to use brushes instead of sticks. And when Gerry had played drums at Beatbox on the song 'Pocket Book Angels', trying to get him to ease off on the fills had been like trying to get London to leave out the guitar solos: a major operation.

During our first song at The Halt I didn't think Richard's drumming was going to go down well with Stuart. I was standing close to the kit on the tiny stage, remembering vividly the time Stuart had stopped a song midway through when Alistair was with us, and all I could really hear was a cymbal. We were playing 'Dog on Wheels', and the cymbal was taking quite a beating, ringing out almost continuously. Stuart had warned David off the cymbals entirely, and I was half expecting him to stop singing at any moment. Richard was fairly thumping the rest of the drums too, but we reached the end of the song and then we played another one. When the set was over I thought that would probably be as much as we played together—but I was wrong. It seemed that from that moment, Richard was in the band.

'The cymbals were pretty loud,' I said to Stuart later, to test his reaction. But he said they were fine.

'He's a great drummer,' Stuart said—so now there were three of us.

9

For the Rhode Island gig at The 13th Note, Stuart rehearsed with each musician individually. We didn't play together as a band until we actually did the show, and I'd never met the flute player until we were standing together in front of the audience.

I rehearsed with Stuart on my own too, but we continued to practise as a trio with London in Beatbox, and we practised as a trio with Richard in the flat a couple of times. I had an ornamental set of bongos my grandma brought back from a holiday. They were made of clay, fired and glazed, with a strange rubber material stretched over them as skins. Richard used those when we practised, tapping them lightly. At Beatbox, the main objective in most of the rehearsals was to try and get London to play an acoustic guitar. The theory was, if we could keep him on acoustic, then we could keep the number of solos down—none of which he was supposed to be playing anyway—and we could try to get him to focus on learning the songs. It wasn't easy. London was a wind-up merchant, and there was nothing he enjoyed more than convincing Stuart he'd finally grasped a song and that he'd decided to play it just as he'd been asked. Then, when Stuart took his eye off him, or softened his voice and his guitar for a gentle part of the song, London would let rip with an insane riff or a clichéd blues solo, and dissolve in a cloud of cackling and knee slaps.

We both knew that, in reality, London could play the songs in his sleep, and that when it came time for the show he'd know them inside out. But trying to make sure he only brought his acoustic guitar to the gig was another matter, and it became a major undertaking.

The room downstairs in The 13th Note was much smaller than the main space, where we'd hosted the Hipster Café Tradefair. There was no stage downstairs, and we set up on the floor, all in a straight line—like a police line-up. Phil Salvin was playing keyboards, but he didn't have a stand for his synth, so he just put it down on the carpet and knelt over it. Mick Cooke played trumpet, Richard sat on a plastic chair with the ornamental bongos on his knee.

There was supposed to be a second support band playing before us but they didn't turn up, so ten minutes before showtime I rehearsed some Raglin Street Rattle songs with Richard and London in the kitchen corridor and we went on and filled that slot. Then it was time for Rhode Island.

London had kept his word and only brought his acoustic guitar, and during the quick set of Raglin Street Rattle songs he'd been as good as gold. But just before Rhode Island were about to start, while we were adjusting microphone stands and Stuart was tuning his guitar, London nudged me and gave me a wink, then he pointed down at the floor. I looked down at his feet, and there, in all its glory, was the biggest effects board I'd ever seen, with a jack lead connecting it to the pickup of his acoustic guitar. And as Stuart counted us in, I nudged Stuart too, and he looked down just in time to see London kicking three of the most extreme-looking pedals into life. Stuart stared in horror as their red LEDs blinked up at him, and off we went into our first song as Rhode Island, on the crashing wave of a monumental guitar solo.

London's infamous cackle rang out continuously during the gig, but overall it went well. It was short—we only played five or six songs—but there were a few Bowlies in the crowd, and it all hung together well for a band who had never played together before. Even so, we never all played together again. It was the only show we did with that line-up, and it was the last time we played with London too. Stuart was carrying his ideal band around in his imagination—and this one wasn't it, so he continued his search.

*

That winter, there was a vicious flu going round the city, and after one particularly frantic day at the flat, I went down with it. The day's activity revolved around a scam that Arlene and Richard had fallen prey to in the morning; some conmen had rented an empty shop unit on Sauchiehall Street for the day, and

93

proceeded to sell empty boxes from it, disguised as bargains. Arlene and Richard had bought a box, but in a twist that was typical of Arlene, she'd taken it back to complain and ended up working in the shop during the afternoon. This led to a big fight with Wee Eric towards evening, followed by Arlene's insistence that she had to get out of town because of some unspecified threat concerning the men she'd been working with. I spent over an hour with her in the train station while she tried to work out what to do and eventually persuaded her to come back to the flat to talk to Eric. Then, after persuading Eric to do the same, and describing to him some of what had happened, I went upstairs to lie down, my legs aching, and I stayed there for the next two weeks.

I had fevers and hallucinations, days asleep and long nights awake, and there were times when I thought it would never end.

While I was ill, Stuart brought me a mixtape he'd made and the songs began to drift through my dreams and my feverish visions. The tape was titled *Winter Aconite*, and he'd made a cover using a film still. On the A-side it said 'Bowlie Compilation', and there were fourteen songs on there, some by bands I'd heard on Karn's mixtapes, some by bands I'd never heard before. This was the track listing:

Salad Days—Young Marble Giants
Veils of Colour—The Blue Aeroplanes
Hours of Darkness Have Changed My Mind—Felt
Ballad of The Times—Everything But The Girl
Almost Prayed—The Weather Prophets

Oomingmak—Cocteau Twins
Sorry For Laughing—Josef K
Brighter—The Railway Children
Outdoor Miner—Wire
Afterglow—The Servants
High Expectation—Stereolab
Savage Sea—The Pop Group
Streets of Your Town—The Go Betweens
City Sickness—Tindersticks

The B-side was Momus' album *Hippopotamomus*. I'd never heard Momus before, but he became my constant companion. Sometimes I couldn't tell if the stereo was still playing him or if it had stopped and I was just hallucinating his songs. For the first week, it was only the need to turn the tape over whenever it ended that got me out of bed, on rubber legs; then I'd fall back in again, exhausted.

As the fever began to subside, though, I also began making the short journey to my desk, and flopping down there to finish off the redrafting of my novel. Then I'd stagger back to the bed again for another hour or two with the mixtape.

By the time the flu was gone, I'd finished the novel and I was left with only one symptom that stayed with me permanently: a rather severe Momus obsession. As soon as my strength returned, I went out to try and find out as much about him as I possibly could.

*

Before Stuart signed up for Beatbox, he'd spent a few

months living in San Francisco, where he'd found a few people to play his music with, and where he'd done a couple of sessions on the radio. Despite having Richard on board for his band now, his frustration at not being able to find the rest of the musicians he was looking for in Glasgow was starting to get to him, and he began talking about going back to San Francisco again. He had the idea that things would start happening for him there, that he'd be able to find the band he was looking for and that people would appreciate his songs in a way they weren't appreciating them at home.

He slowly grew more serious about the idea, and I started to get concerned that I'd miss out on the melody writing lessons he'd promised to give me. For a while now I'd been trying to fix up an arrangement with him involving the piano rooms in the Mitchell Library, but I realised that if he left for San Francisco like he was planning to do, I'd miss out completely.

I hoped it wouldn't happen.

*

With my novel completed in those final days of the flu, I printed out the manuscript I'd typed up on my Atari ST and started sending it out to publishers with high hopes. I'd written two novels before this one, and sent them both out to every publisher in the UK, but apart from a few of them requesting the full manuscript and giving me encouraging comments, nothing had happened. The first one had been judged too uncommercial for anyone to publish, although it got close with Penguin. The second—which I'd finished when I was twenty-two—had been deemed too whimsical by the editors who had liked the first one. They felt it lacked the first one's 'visceral quality'.

But this time things would be different, I decided. I'd found a voice with the third one, and I'd had my short story published in the HarperCollins anthology now, alongside Ali Smith, Candia McWilliam and Iain Crichton Smith. And on top of that I had a new magic weapon: Arlene, who was pretending to be my literary agent, complete with headed notepaper and her winning ways.

I called the novel *Nalda Said* and we typed up Arlene's letter of recommendation, then we started sending it out.

Nothing happened.

Nothing happened with the Raglin Street Rattle tape I gave to Richard to take in to his music business course either. I'd given it to him as soon as they were open to submissions, but he stayed suspiciously quiet about it whenever we spoke after that. Eventually, I asked him if it had got anywhere and he told me it hadn't got through the first round of listens.

Even though Raglin Street Rattle didn't exist any more I was still disappointed. One morning at breakfast I said to Richard that I thought I needed to change the style of my singing voice. After a short pause Richard told me he didn't think I needed to change my voice.

'You just need to change what you're doing with it,' he said, which didn't really help the way I was feeling.

What with nothing happening with *Nalda Said*, and my music having reached the point where I no longer had a band, I started to wonder if there wasn't maybe a San Francisco of my own I could set out for, where things might start to happen for me. It seemed I was in the same situation as Stuart—we were both doing everything we could, but neither of us could make anything happen. We were sending our work out into the world and watching it being ignored or rejected, before it limped back home again.

It had got so that I couldn't even beat Iain at Connect Four in our long evening sessions at the kitchen table. I started to suspect Iain had a system of some kind, a secret piece of knowledge that I didn't have. And as we played I started to think there must be some secret piece of knowledge in general that I didn't have. I thought of the rent I paid to my landlord to sit in this kitchen, with six other people paying him the same rent to sit there too. And I thought of all the kitchens he owned across the city. I thought of the people running Beatbox, and all the money they were rumoured to be getting to keep us sitting in there to help fund their studio. And I thought of all the years I'd been working for, and the £56 a week I was living on. Surely there was something these other people knew? How could I find that out? How could I make something happen? How could I get a line of four yellow discs amongst Iain's red ones, and win at Connect Four?

At the time, it didn't even feel like the calm before the storm, the still point before everything starts—it just felt like an unbeatable trap.

*

We eventually found out what the Beatbox management had been manufacturing in the constantly locked studio control room, and it wasn't a spaceship at all. It turned out, in fact, to be a boy band. John McLaughlin—one of the few members from the band on the posters who was still hanging about—was writing the songs, while Alan Rankine whisked in and out bringing reports of the buzz he was whipping up in the industry, and issuing orders when things were needed suddenly and unexpectedly to back up some of the claims he'd been making.

The boy band themselves never seemed to be there. There was a rumour that they were from Newcastle, and only ever came in at weekends when the course was closed. But we did see them once, being hurried up through the corridor with towels thrown over their heads to hide their identities. Before they reached the studio, though, they removed the towels, and they drew a stark contrast with the musicians on the course, the lazy figures sitting on the floor with their backs up against the wall, or lying on the punctured sofas dotted about the place. They seemed to have come from a different world, a world of airbrushing and plastic moulding. It was as if they already existed in the world of photographs, even though they were there in the corridor.

And then they were gone, ushered into the sanctuary of the control room, and we all agreed that they were going nowhere, destined to disappear into the same oblivion as the band in the posters on the wall.

Their name was 911.

Over the next five years they sold ten million records.

10

When the storm began, it began quietly. With a whisper. With a rumour. We began to hear mutterings that Stuart's Rhode Island tape was getting a good response from the students at Stow College, on Richard's course.

One afternoon at Beatbox Alan Rankine hurried past us in the corridor and said, 'You're Rhode Island? My class are liking your tape.'

Then I heard from Richard that it was down to two bands; that the class were fighting over whether they should choose Rhode Island or Motorlife Co. to make the single for them. Richard said Motorlife Co. were in front, and likely to win, but he said there was a chance. Over the next few days we started to hear reports that it was becoming more of an even contest, and somebody suggested to us—possibly Richard, possibly Alan Rankine—that we should go into the class and play for them, to try and tip things in our favour.

Stuart was still intent on heading off to San Francisco for the foreseeable future, but he decided we should go into the class and play them some songs anyway, and one afternoon, taking our guitars and my personal stereo speakers for Stuart to sing through, we walked up the hill behind my flat and down the other side to Stow College, both of us wearing silver trousers—Stuart's plastic, mine velvet.

The reception when we got there was different from what we'd been expecting. It turned out that most of the class had already decided they wanted us to do the single—and our run-through of a few songs, with Mick Cooke playing trumpet and Richard sitting quietly at his desk pretending he had nothing to do with the band, only seemed to make them more keen, personal stereo speakers and all. A couple of the boys in the class remained non-committal, but most of the others told us then and there we could do the single.

'We'll see how it goes,' Alan Rankine said, then he thanked us for coming and we walked up and down the hill again.

Over the next couple of weeks the whispers grew more and more positive, to the extent that Gordon Rintoul, who had always just been a blur to us before, asked to talk to us in the studio—where he offered to be Stuart's manager. It was something of a turnaround—after having been on his course for more than a year, and having our music routinely ignored by him. But Stuart turned him down. Gordon told him to think it over, and I thought while we were in the meeting he might accept, but as soon as Gordon left Stuart told me it wasn't going to happen—that Gordon couldn't take him where he wanted to go. And even though we'd always been unimpressed with the bands Gordon was managing, and none of them had got anywhere in particular, I was still impressed by Stuart's certainty that he could do better, and by the fact that he didn't even consider it. Especially when he was so keen for something to start happening for him.

But I was even more surprised when the rumours of him being offered the Stow College single began to turn into whispers that it was going to happen, and he told me he wouldn't be able to do it. He was sticking with his plan of going to San Francisco. One morning in the kitchen Richard told me that the class had come to an agreement, finally, that they wanted Rhode Island to make the single, and I told him it probably wouldn't happen because Stuart was leaving Glasgow.

Neither of us could understand his decision.

With time running out for my melody lessons, I raised the subject one more time with Stuart, and tried to fix up a date for the Mitchell Library. We were walking towards Charing Cross, on the pavements high above the motorway, but instead of making an appointment Stuart just told me everything he knew about the subject, then and there.

'Melodies just happen,' he said. 'They just pop into your head sometimes. All you have to do is listen.'

And he told me that it was all about training yourself to become aware that the melodies were there, lurking quietly in the background, and then working out the chords on guitar to accompany them.

Brief though it was, my single 'lesson' was a

revelation for me. When I'd been fourteen or fifteen, and planning to become a songwriter, I'd often just started singing a tune I found in my head. It was something I'd always done, prior to that. I could remember being three or four, lying in bed singing songs to myself about a rabbit or about Snow White, following the tune wherever it went, while I told myself a bewildering story. But when I'd got my first keyboard, at fifteen, determined to put my plan of escape into action, I found I didn't know how to work out the chords and arrangements to accompany the melodies I was singing. I realised I could only go about things by writing the chord sequence first, then building the song up from there. I didn't know enough about music theory to know I only needed to learn a little bit more to let me harmonise and arrange the melodies that came naturally to me—so I stopped paying attention to the tunes in my head altogether.

'A melody is always stronger if it comes before the chord sequence,' Stuart told me. 'If you start out with the chord sequence, it restricts where the tune can go.'

So with Stuart's advice, I started paying attention to the melodies that popped into my head again. I bought a Dictaphone and carried it in my pocket all the time, keeping it beside my bed when I went to sleep at night and occasionally singing into it when I woke up with a tune in my head. I'd stop on the street sometimes too, when I found a quiet spot with no one else around, to record a fragment I'd found repeating itself over and over while I walked. It seemed to be a never-ending source, and the more attention I paid to it the more the melodies came. It was as if the very act of recording the melodies gave them the confidence to come forward, gave them permission to evolve and appear. And the best thing of all was that I now knew enough about music to work out the chords on guitar to accompany them, and to turn them into bits of songs.

It was the beginning of something new. I was only writing fragments—I still couldn't work out how to develop them into complete songs—but it was a start, and I imagined this would be my main project from now on. Without my own band, with my novel finished and with my days of playing bass with Stuart coming to an end, it looked like I was going to have plenty of time to figure it all out—to just listen to the music in my head and hope the songs got longer and more complete as time went on. I sat my Atari ST next to the four-track in my room—hooking them together with a MIDI cable, making sure I was ready and waiting when the good stuff arrived.

And then things went slightly pear-shaped.

With a firm offer to record the Stow College single on the table, Stuart began to ask me searching questions. He remained committed to his San Francisco trip, but he asked if I thought the opportunities that were starting to appear for him in Glasgow would still be there waiting when he came back. He seemed convinced they would be. I told him I wasn't so sure.

'Sometimes you only get one shot,' I told him. 'It's easy just to miss your chance.'

Richard felt the same. He was certain that if you didn't grab your break when it appeared, it might never come again. He couldn't believe Stuart was going off to

San Francisco rather than making the single for Stow.

So Stuart, still unconvinced but willing to look into things further, set up another meeting with the class and we went in to talk to them—wearing normal trousers this time.

It was a novelty for us to see Alan Rankine standing still, rather than rushing past in a blur in the Beatbox corridor. He wrote some stuff on the whiteboard to illustrate what the process would involve, and he wrote some dates up there too. The budget would cover five days in Cava Studios. Three for recording, two for mixing. We'd record a single and a B-side in February, and then the class would act as a record label called Electric Honey and release a thousand copies of the single on CD and promote it. Alan explained that the main purpose of it was to give the students experience of everything that was involved in putting out a record, but that it would be a good thing for us too because we would get some publicity from it and it might generate a bit of a buzz for the band.

The first thing Stuart made clear was his opposition to releasing a CD.

'Singles have to be vinyl,' he said. 'Seven inch.'

He explained that a seven-inch single was a magical thing, and that CDs were nothing at all.

Alan hesitated, but he eventually said we could probably do it on vinyl, if we really wanted to.

Stuart gave that some thought then shook his head.

'I don't know,' he said. 'How about if we made an album? I think it has to be an album.'

The pause before Alan replied this time was a lot longer, and he finally told us he didn't think it could be done. Not in five days.

'Five days are plenty,' Stuart replied, and he went up to the whiteboard and wiped a space amongst Alan's doodlings. Then he picked up the marker pen and started writing song titles on the board. 'The State I Am In', 'Expectations', 'She's Losing It'; five in one list on the left-hand side of the board, and five in another list on the right-hand side. When he was finished he turned back to look at Alan as if that was all the proof that was needed.

I was getting used to Stuart's ability to get what he wanted where his songs were concerned, but this seemed like a bridge too far. Most of the class were excited by the idea, staring at the whiteboard with wide eyes and smiles on their faces—all except for Richard, who looked a bit seasick. But Alan wasn't convinced. He told Stuart it really wasn't enough time, that you couldn't record an album in three days. Stuart told him how quickly The Beatles had made their first few albums, and told him we'd record it all live, no overdubs. It went back and forward for a while, punctuated by visits from Stuart to the whiteboard to write something down. And then, quite suddenly, Alan changed his mind. He decided to give Stuart the chance to make the album. I'm not sure if even Alan believed what had just happened.

After the debate was over, and Stuart was talking to some of the students, Alan told me Stuart's attitude reminded him of Billy McKenzie, the singer in The Associates.

'Bill always knew what he wanted,' he said. 'Great artists usually do. You have to give them room to follow their vision.'

And so Stuart cancelled his trip to San Francisco.

11

In Beatbox there were three guys who were always together—David Semple and the two Pauls. They came as a package deal, you either saw all three of them or you didn't see them at all, and whenever they participated in a task they stayed together on the sidelines, like a community set apart.

Outwardly, they didn't have much in common. Paul One always wore combat trousers and army boots, with a bright orange waterproof coat that he never took off. He had a big round shaved head and a goatee beard, and he played in a speed-something-or-other band. Paul Two was rechristened Macca, to differentiate him from Paul One. He dressed in black and kept his hair slick. He played in a band who were influenced by New Order and The Clash, and he was always being ribbed by the other two for being world-weary—for having been there and done that—partly because he was already married with two kids. David Semple was something of an enigma. He didn't play a musical instrument and he wasn't in any band. No one was quite sure how he'd managed to get on the course in the first place, and how he'd managed to stay now that he was here. But he had a witty comment for everything that occurred in Beatbox, and he lit the place up a bit.

The three of them had originally come together to run the record label that had been set up as part of the course before I joined. I'd submitted a tape to them right at the beginning, so had Stuart, but our tapes had gotten nowhere. They'd advertised for demos to be submitted out in the real world too, and one afternoon I heard them laughing together about a reference one of them made to a song one of my friends had sent in. I'd always thought it was a great song, but it became one of their in-jokes for a while.

Eventually, they signed a band called The Diggers from Glasgow, on the strength of the buzz that was circulating about them. I don't think any of them liked The Diggers, but Gordon Rintoul had convinced them it was a good move—and that was one of my first insights into how the music business worked, even at a tiny level. Until then, I'd always thought record companies found bands they liked and promoted them to the public. Here, I was seeing something else entirely: a record company looking for bands that already had already built an audience, and signing them up to sell records to that fanbase.

So Paul, Macca and Semple had recorded two songs by The Diggers in the Beatbox studio, and then pressed up a few hundred CD singles. Before they even had time to release the single, though, Creation signed The

110

Diggers to a proper recording contract, offering to make a payment to the Beatbox label to stop the single being released. And now the office that had been assigned to the three amigos was piled high with unsold CDs, and they were destined to wander around the dark corridors aimlessly, bound together by their failed enterprise, forever waiting for the payment from Creation that never seemed to come.

In its absence, and unable to carry on any record company business without it, their main occupation became the revival of wit and wordplay as it had been practised by the Victorian aesthetes. Sitting listening to them, they seemed to have created their own world made entirely of linguistic quirks and in-jokes. At any given moment, one of them might say something as simple as the name of a film star—'Natalie Wood'—then the next one would continue with 'James Caan'. 'Brian Cant,' the third one would say, and eventually you would realise they were listing names of the famous whose surnames worked as auxiliary verbs, making it sound as if they were commenting on whether or not these people would participate in some mysterious venture they'd proposed. 'Will Carling?' 'Brian May', 'Walt Disney' (Disney being the proper Scottish pronunciation of 'doesn't'). Inmates became wary of saying anything at all in their company, well aware that the simplest sentence was likely to be picked apart, rephrased, riffed upon and then sent back to you with a meaning entirely the opposite of the one you had intended—usually one that made you out to be a pervert or a numbskull.

It was a world that could easily draw you in,

especially when most of the other goings-on in Beatbox were uniformly dull. But it was also easy to forget that no one outside of Beatbox shared the frame of reference—and it was this combination of factors that led to my first misjudged encounter with Stevie Jackson.

Stuart had continued to try out new songs in The Halt Bar, and I'd continued to go along and watch him doing it. It was in The Halt Bar I first heard 'She's Losing It', and as the melody lifted up into the chorus, and then bounced back down on the other side again, I realised Stuart had written an almost perfect song. I kept waiting for it to let me down, for the tune not to deliver the twists it had promised, or to fall flat on its face, but it didn't happen. It kept living up to its own brilliant standards, all the way to the end. And when it finished, to a smattering of applause in the half-empty afternoon bar, I felt sure I'd never seen an unknown songwriter singing such a fully realised song before. I'd seen hundreds of aspiring songwriters over the years, in The Halt and in Beatbox and at the songwriters' night at Blackfriars in the Merchant City. I'd heard demos and watched unsigned bands and collaborated with a lot of songwriters myself, but it was clear to me now that none of them had actually known what they were doing. They'd all been 'trying' to write a song, but Stuart had actually written one.

Stevie Jackson from The Moondials was in The Halt that afternoon, and he was there the next time we played as a trio, with Richard on drums. That night was busier, a midweek gathering, and at the end of the night, when most of the audience had gone home, we were standing outside talking to some other singers who had done open mic spots, when Stevie came outside with The Usual Suspects. We were blocking the pavement by then, and Stevie tried to get a bit closer.

'I wanted to tell you I really like your songs,' he said to Stuart—and that was when I made my blunder. It seemed like the perfect opportunity to unleash the phrase of the moment from Beatbox. Whenever anyone in there had paid anyone else a compliment during the past few weeks, one of the Pauls—or David Semple—had unfailingly been on hand to respond with the quip, 'If you want to shag him, you should just ask him out.'

And so, in their absence, I did the honours myself.

It didn't go down well. Stevie looked at me coolly without responding, held me in his gaze for a few uncomfortable seconds and then went back to talking to Stuart again. He told Stuart he'd watched him playing in The Halt a few times now, and that he'd always enjoyed it. Stuart, being a fan of Stevie's guitar playing, told him about the record he was about to make and asked Stevie if he would be in the band. Stevie said he didn't want to be in a band again, but he told Stuart he should get in touch with him about playing on the record. He said he would do that.

'You should join the band,' Stuart told him, but Stevie shook his head and then we went our separate ways, Stuart wondering how to get Stevie to change his mind, and me resolving to leave Beatbox witticisms at the door of the building in future.

As word spread around Glasgow that Stuart was going to be making an album, a curious thing started to happen. Suddenly, after years of not being able to find any musicians to play on his songs, almost everybody

113

wanted to be in his band. Just a few weeks after he'd planned to leave for San Francisco because nothing was happening for him, people all over the city began to approach him and ask if they could play on his album. Musicians in Beatbox, musicians in The 13th Note, musicians in The Halt Bar: people who'd always been there and never paid much notice before. I watched Stuart nod at them and make no further response. For the most part, they still didn't fit with the picture he had for his ideal band, but the fact that they'd never said anything positive about his songs in the past wasn't lost on him either. For the time being, there was still only one more person he wanted to add to the line-up, and that was Stevie.

One afternoon, I came home from Beatbox to find Richard sitting at the kitchen table with one of the boys from his course. He turned out to be one of the few who'd been pushing for Motorlife Co. to do the single instead of Rhode Island. His name was Neil. Richard introduced us and we talked about a few things, but he didn't stay for long. I thought it was probably because he was still annoyed that Motorlife Co. had lost out to us, but I later found out that the story was quite different.

As well as being a student on the Stow College course, Neil was doing some regional A&R scouting for a new record company in London called Jeepster. He went to gigs, kept up with the bands that were getting good word of mouth in Glasgow, and then let Jeepster know about the ones he thought it was worth listening to. It turned out he'd already heard Stuart's demo tape before it was submitted to the Stow College course. He'd heard it being played on the radio, on Beat Patrol, and he'd told Jeepster that they should sign Rhode Island. Then, when Stuart's tape became popular with the rest of the class, Neil had attempted to convince the course to go with Motorlife Co. instead, so that Rhode Island could sign to Jeepster and Neil would get his commission for finding them.

I'm not sure how convinced Jeepster had been by Neil's recommendation, but it seemed that—like was happening with a lot of other people—the news that we had been chosen to make the record for Electric Honey got them interested, and it wasn't long until we started to hear whispers that Mark Jones, the head of Jeepster, wanted to meet us.

*

When Stevie Jackson was in The Moondials, they'd done everything a band could do. They'd lived together like The Monkees, they'd practised and written night and day. They'd toured in a beaten-up van all over Europe, busking on the streets of foreign cities to pay for their food and their petrol; they'd even recorded and released a single with the Electric Honey label. But apart from a bit of airplay, nothing had happened for them—and all that living together had taken its toll on their relationships with each other, and they'd decided to call it a day.

Stevie's experience with The Moondials was the main reason he didn't want to be in another band. He'd seen everything that could happen to people when they were in a band together, and he didn't want to go through it all again. He didn't want the disappointment and the arguments, sleeping in freezing cold vans and not eating for days at a time. So he stood his ground— he'd play guitar on Stuart's album, but he wouldn't join the band.

The first time we arranged to rehearse at his flat I got there before Stuart, and Stevie was drinking Lemsip and Night Nurse because he had a cold. He was living in a long attic room, up near the university, and he said Stuart had phoned to say he'd be late. I still felt awkward about the Beatbox remark I'd made outside The Halt, and I wished Stuart had got there before me, but I'd seen Stevie playing in The Halt enough times to know we both loved Bob Dylan—so I talked to him about *Blonde On Blonde*. I asked him some stuff about The Moondials too, and about the single they'd made for Electric Honey, but Stuart still didn't turn up.

I was used to meeting new people almost every day at the flat and in Beatbox. There was always someone I didn't know sitting in the kitchen or being thrown into the computer room, and although I'd always been shy of meeting new people I'd developed a few techniques to help me through recently. None of them worked on Stevie, though. Whenever I tried to turn something into a joke he didn't laugh, and I got the feeling he wondered what I was doing there, babbling away, when he'd arranged to meet up with Stuart to learn some of his songs.

As we talked, though, one thing became abundantly clear to me: Stevie was hugely impressed by Stuart's songwriting. I'd played with a lot of people on Stuart's

116

songs over the past year, but nobody—except maybe Alistair from Lisa Helps the Blind—had been half as impressed by them as Stevie was. He could already play fragments of them, just from hearing them in The Halt, and he talked about them with a kind of awe. I showed him some of the sections he wasn't sure about, and as he played, one more thing became clear to me: none of the guitarists we'd worked with before could hold a candle to Stevie. He could do just about anything, and it was all free of the rock and blues clichés that even the best guitarists we'd played with had been in thrall to. Stevie's playing was pure shimmering pop. And in stark contrast to London, he rarely went for a solo.

I sat on the floor, looking through some of his records while he went off to answer the phone—trying to think up something else to talk about when he came back. But it was Stuart on the phone, saying he wasn't going to make it after all. Saying he'd been held up somewhere. And when I'd finished showing Stevie the chorus for 'The State I Am In', I packed up my bass and went home, a bit bewildered by the encounter, and feeling very shy.

I didn't realise at the time that Stevie was shy too.

12

There were two clauses in the lease for our flat that were written in bold and underlined. The first said no overnight guests were allowed, the second simply said: Strictly No Parties. From the moment Wee Eric had arrived in Glasgow he'd been an almost permanent overnight guest at our place. As far as Arlene was concerned, the terms of the lease were simply challenges—and she soon set her sights on overcoming the second one too, by planning to throw the biggest and best party the city had ever seen.

'My parties are legendary,' she told us, and got round our objections to her plan by setting a date and starting to invite people—beginning with the entire population of Eric's house up at the Art School. With that done, resistance was futile. Everywhere she went she invited more people, and she encouraged us to do the same. She told us people would be talking about this party for years to come, that it would go down in history, and I started planning to be out of town on the arranged date.

Richard had similar ideas. We listened to Arlene waxing lyrical about her party in the kitchen at night, and outlined our escape plans at breakfast in the mornings. Invites soon totalled more than a hundred, without anyone else having invited anyone, and it was starting to look like the most probable outcome would be the complete destruction of the place, with no need for any evictions. We continued to work on our alibis, and just about had them in order when Arlene found a way to turn the tables on us. One evening, when Stuart was visiting, and being given a florid description of how fantastic this party would be, she suddenly stopped mid-sentence and hit him on the arm.

'You should play at it,' she shouted. She jumped up and hit me and Richard too. 'You should all play at it. Your band should play at the party.' She was so excited by her idea she could hardly contain herself, and Stuart became infected by her madness. He agreed we would do it, with Stevie too, and we watched as our escape plans went up in smoke.

*

Even though we would only have three days of recording to make the album for Stow College, which would mean doing live takes for most of the songs with very little overdubbing, Stuart didn't seem in any rush to get us rehearsing as a band. He stuck with the system he'd employed for the 13th Note show, rehearsing with each musician individually, just him and them, quite often teaching them a part he'd written himself. Occasionally, I rehearsed with him and Richard at the same time, with Richard playing the ornamental set of bongos rather than an actual drum kit, but most of the time when I played the new songs for the album it was just the two of us—Stuart and me—in my room or in the empty songwriting room at Beatbox. I slowly learned 'Expectations', 'She's Losing It', 'Mary Jo'. And sometimes when we were playing through them we'd ask David Semple to come into the songwriting room to listen, to let us know what he thought. Most of the time he would just nod sagely.

While we rehearsed, Stuart began to talk about a short story he was writing. I'd recently let him read my novel, and he said he wanted to know what I thought of his story when it was ready. He started making trips to the Mitchell Library to work on it, and when it was finished and typed up he spent a while working on a cover for it. When I finally got a copy it was presented in a similar way to the programmes he'd made up for the Lisa Helps the Blind gig we'd done in Alistair's front room. The typed pages were held together with a plastic spine and a clear acetate page sat on top of the red cover page, which had a monochrome photograph of a boy and a girl on it.

The story was called 'Belle and Sebastian'.

I've never liked reading other people's unpublished stories. For a while, when I was writing short stories myself, I went to a creative writing class in Maryhill with my friend Dougie, who was also a writer. I don't think either of us really knew why we were going there after the first visit. It was a terrible gathering of seething jealousies and towering narcissism. Everyone there was convinced that their genius was so magnificent it was incomprehensible to anyone else but themselves and the one all-powerful critic who would one day discover them. And everyone believed that everyone else in the group was a pedlar of trashy, self-indulgent nonsense, who was only taking up some of the time and attention that should rightfully be allocated to their own work. The tutor's own short stories regularly appeared in a small Scottish literary magazine where he held an editorial role, and he encouraged us to sit in a circle and read our stories to each other, then comment on them. The whole experience had given me a recurring feeling of trauma whenever someone asked me to read their stories or listen to their poetry, and it was something I always took pains to avoid.

Stuart's story was about an older boy teaching a younger girl who was still at school how to play guitar, and it reminded me of Momus' song 'The Guitar Lesson'. The story mainly involved the boy going to the girl's house when she finished school, and then talking to her about other things while he was supposed to be teaching her guitar. The characters inhabited the same universe as most of the characters in his new songs—songs like 'Expectations', 'You're Just a Baby', 'She's Losing It'—and I wondered what kept drawing him back to that time in life. I could tell, though, that the story had got to the heart of something for him. And although the rhythm of the prose sometimes gave me flashbacks to those traumatic nights in Maryhill, it was clear that—with the completion of 'Belle and Sebastian'—Stuart had defined the imaginary

121

landscape his work would exist within. It was a statement of intent; almost a manifesto. And, in the title, he'd found a new name for his band.

*

Every now and again, there was a sudden panic at Beatbox amongst the staff. It would originate in the main office, and filter down to us through Neil Cameron, the Cubase tutor. The general theme was usually to do with the inmates lack of discipline and motivation, often with a minor variation such as timekeeping or attendance thrown in for good measure. A meeting would be called and the corridor would fill up with bodies, then Gordon Rintoul, the head of operations, would occasionally appear, although more often the task of trying to whip up some enthusiasm and establish a new structure would fall to his wife Allison, loyally accompanied by Neil.

We'd be informed that Beatbox was in danger of losing its funding because of the lack of evidence available to the council that we were actually doing anything or learning anything on the course. And the meeting would begin as an attack on the course inmates. We'd be berated for our lack of drive, refusal to keep diaries, failure to attend classes. Various inmates would then point out that there were no classes for us to attend, that there wasn't enough equipment for everyone to be working at once, that the studio was mostly locked and occupied by the commercial projects. Frustrated, the tutors would then get annoyed that we weren't just doing stuff, fulfilling the brief that we were meant to fulfil—and the end result was that a few more bodies would secretly decide it was time to leave the course and just not come back again, while the shrunken number of us that were left would be treated to a focused project for the next couple of weeks, until it all gradually unravelled and everything went back to the way it had been before.

After one particularly serious get-together, the task we were assigned involved us forming into large groups to write a song and carry it all the way through to recording it in the studio. I had a guitar riff, and six or seven of us assembled round one acoustic guitar while I played it over and over, hoping someone else would come up with a way to develop it. It had a vocal part too, that went 'Bah-bah-rah, bah-bah-bah-bah-rah', but no one had any ideas. For the next few days, whenever anyone from the office came out to make sure we were adhering to the new regime, the seven of us would form a circle around the guitar and I'd bash out the riff again, till whoever it was walked past nodding and disappeared into the office again. Sometimes I kept playing it for a little while after they'd gone, in the fading hope that a new part would appear—and one afternoon, when I was just about to stop, Stuart, who wasn't a part of our group, walked past and said,

'I think I can hear a verse.'

He covered his ears and started humming to himself, then he took the guitar into another room for a few minutes. When he came back he put one foot up on a chair and propped the guitar on his knee. He started playing around four chords, then hummed the melody: one opening line followed by a second line that repeated

123

three times. He repeated the whole thing twice to make two verses out of it, then merged it into my chorus riff part at the end, and it worked. It fitted. He recorded it onto my Dictaphone so's we wouldn't forget it. Then he handed me the guitar back, put his jacket on and went home.

Over the next couple of days I worked on finding a second part to add onto my riff, another half to turn it into a full chorus and lead back to the verse again. Slowly, I got an idea of what it should do, then when I was fully frustrated I gathered the group together in Beatbox, to see if anyone could come up with the kind of thing I was imagining. I played the riff and then said, 'It needs something a bit like this –'

I went into the chord sequence I'd been trying out, and hummed along with it and asked them if they had any ideas.

'It sounds like you've already got it,' Paul Two said.

'Just do that?' I asked him.

Everyone shrugged and Paul said, 'It sounds good enough to me.'

Then Andy, who was exclusively into death metal, said there should be a chugging minor chord between the opening riff and the first verse, and he played it on the guitar. And musically, that was the song finished. I said I'd write some words for it, and the group dispersed until it was time to record.

It was a joy writing words for Stuart's melody, and I didn't rush it. I wandered the streets over the next few days with his tune playing in my head, letting different lyrics come and go—relishing the potential of the thing without committing to anything. It seemed like a long time since I'd written the words for a song, and I remembered this was what I'd done with the tunes I'd written with David Campbell too—walked in the park, feeling a freedom in all the possibilities that lay before me. There was something special about Stuart's melody, though. It brought forth more words than usual. All kinds of couplets and phrases, ideas that would never have occurred to me without the tune.

Eventually, though, a finished form began to emerge, leaving fewer and fewer lines blank, like it always does, and one night Stuart came round to the flat and I let him hear the finished thing. I played it on acoustic guitar, and afterwards he said that first time through the chorus, when I'd gone into my new section after the riff, he'd thought it was about to go somewhere special. The first two chords of that part, and the first line of the melody, had made him think something good was about to happen, but it hadn't happened—it hadn't gone to that special place he'd been expecting.

I asked him if he could make it go there. I told him I'd wanted it to go somewhere else, and that I'd only put in the bit I had as an example to the rest of the group, hoping one of them could work out where it should go, until Paul Two had told me I'd cracked it, and it was fine as it was.

I played the part for Stuart again, hoping he could work out how to make it do what he thought it should do, but he couldn't. He said he didn't know what should happen, just that the first line of the chorus had made him think something special was about to happen. I asked him if he wanted to try and work on it himself, on his own, but he didn't, and so we left it as it was. Stuart said his favourite line in the lyrics was a line in the verse—where I'd changed the melody a bit—where it said, 'And someone called/From an upstairs window/"Mister, let the past go."'

When he went home, I played the chorus over and over, leaving the guitar down then going back to it for the rest of the night—each time hoping that what he'd thought should happen would accidentally happen on one of my run-throughs, but it didn't. I hummed the tune to myself in the shower, trying to imagine other places it could go at that point, but nothing appeared.

And so, a couple of days later in Beatbox, we recorded the song in the studio to complete the task we'd been given. I called it 'Falling Down', and when it was finished the old order gradually returned to Beatbox, and we went back to knocking about in the same way we'd done before the frantic meeting.

Even so, not too long after that frantic meeting, the numbers attending Beatbox began to dwindle. When inmates left at the end of their six-month sentence, no one new would come in to replace them. It seemed that the project to build the spaceship by cramming as many people onto the course as possible had been abandoned, and things became a bit more agreeable. Gradually, there was almost enough oxygen for each person to breathe for a whole day, and you could get on a computer whenever you wanted, or make use of the piano in the music room whenever you felt like it.

During this exodus, with their patience in waiting for the money from Creation exhausted, both Pauls left the course. Paul One first, to work at a promotions

126

company, and Paul Two a few weeks later, leaving David Semple to continue their witty legacy single-handed. David held out some hope for the record label to begin with, but quite quickly Gordon told him that they were shutting it down. The Creation money, when it came, would be put to other uses—and Semple, still uninterested in playing or composing music, but determined not to leave, took to spending his days touring the various sofas spread throughout the labyrinth, smoking two or three cigarettes on each one before moving on, and echoing fragments of catchphrases and word games he'd once shared with the two Pauls, whenever they could be applied to the events happening around him.

The sofa where he was most likely to be found was the one in the main office, a sofa off limits to regular inmates. Because of Semple's earlier association with the record label he had some VIP status, and he spent so much time in the office that he was eventually given some vague administrative responsibility, which he didn't bother to fulfil. Instead, he spent most of his time fiddling about on the burgeoning internet, with Neil's suitcase-sized laptop—and in particular, hunting around on Momus' website.

Semple was another Momus fan, an obsessive on the same level as I had become since Stuart brought me the mixtapes when I was ill. Momus was probably one of the first artists to have his own website, and he was certainly one of the first to have his songs on there. Or at least clips of his songs, which even at thirty seconds long stretched the internet to the limit of its capabilities in 1995. Semple's patience for sitting on the sofa in the office, quietly smoking cigarettes, was infinite—and it needed to be for the specific task of listening to the clips on Momus' website. When I found out what he was doing in there, I decided I had to get in on it too, and I got permission from Neil to have internet lessons. This involved me sitting on the sofa beside Semple, while Neil's laptop sat on a desk in a far-off corner of the room, plugged into the phone line and blocking all incoming and outgoing calls to and from the office, while we waited upwards of a quarter of an hour for our next Momus clip to download.

We were addicts, anxious to find clips of songs we'd never heard before, and it didn't matter that the quality was so low they sounded as if they were being played to us over the telephone in the 1920s, or that each one cost more to download in phone bill charges than it would have cost to buy the whole album in a shop. We lived for those thirty seconds of lo-fi magic, sent to us by science fiction from the future, when each one had to be erased from the hard drive before the next one was downloaded because there wasn't enough memory to store two of them at once.

13

While I was splitting my days between sitting on the office sofa with Semple and rehearsing my bass parts with Stuart in the music room, we started to hear rumours that a buzz was circulating in the music business about Rhode Island, even though Rhode Island still wasn't a band yet. I think Alan Rankine had got the buzz going, to lay the groundwork for the Electric Honey record when it came out. But the record company boss who was the most buzzed, and the first to make contact with us, was the one Neil from the Stow College course had been doing A&R for. Mark Jones from Jeepster Records was desperate to see us playing live—and since we had no proper shows planned before recording the album, Stuart invited Mark to come and see us play at Arlene's party.

With this new incentive to put on a proper show, the four of us—Richard, Stevie, Stuart and me—began to rehearse more regularly together. Sometimes in the flat, with Richard on the ornamental bongos and Stuart singing through the personal stereo speakers—which was exactly how we planned to do the show—and once or twice in a rehearsal room with a full drum kit, which we counted as rehearsing for the album.

And then, a couple of weeks before the party, Stuart said he'd found two more musicians he thought could be perfect for the band. The first one was a cello player he'd met at a party. Her name was Isobel—her friends called her Bel—and because Stuart had just written his Belle and Sebastian story, he took it as a sign. He said it was fate; Isobel was exactly the kind of musician he'd been looking for to make his band complete. He'd even started referring to his band as Belle and Sebastian lately. But one night, after meeting up with Isobel a couple of times, he came round to my flat very dejected, almost as dejected as he'd been when he planned to leave for San Francisco.

'You write a short story,' he said. 'And you expect it to come true. You expect it to happen the way you've imagined it, but…'

And that was all he said about it. But before he left he'd resolved not to give up hope; to keep believing that Isobel was perfect for his band, and that it was fated to be. And, in the meantime, it was the other musician he'd discovered that I was introduced to first.

I came home one night and he was sitting in Richard's room with Stuart.

'This is Chris,' Stuart said. 'He plays keyboards.'

Chris was incredibly young. He was wearing vintage glasses and a black leather jacket, and he seemed a bit frightened, but I was impressed by the ability he had just to be himself, without pretending to be cool, without pretending to know things he didn't know. It struck me as unusual in someone so young. During that first meeting I remember Chris being preoccupied with the way he was storing his records at home, the sleeves they were in. I don't know if it was a preoccupation he had brought with him or if it had been inspired by the sight of Richard's substantial record collection which lined the walls of the tiny room, but it was causing him quite a bit of anguish now that it had taken hold. And even though Stuart talked about the band and the plans he had for it, and Chris talked briefly about different kinds of keyboards and what he would like to contribute if he could, the meeting ended with Chris coming to the conclusion that there were no shortcuts to the problem he was having with his record collection, and he was going to have to buy a protective sleeve for every record he owned, something he'd been hoping he wouldn't have to do.

Much later, I took part in an interview where Chris told the interviewer that one of the most difficult things about making an album was that you always felt your record collection was sitting looking over your shoulder, judging everything you did in comparison to itself. At that first meeting, it was clear that his record collection occupied most of his thoughts, informing the way he dressed and the way he talked, and the level of his dedication to it and the way it deeply informed his life was impressive and inspiring.

Despite Stuart's disillusionment after his first meetings with Isobel, things began to look up quite quickly. He was soon rehearsing with her for the album, convinced that his initial hunch about her had been right. He rehearsed with Chris on his own too. It was only Stevie, Stuart, Richard and me who ever rehearsed together before the gig at the party.

On the afternoon of the party we met up with Mark Jones in our favourite café, the Grosvenor on Ashton Lane.

The Grosvenor Café was a magical place—the heart of the west end for musicians and artists and writers at that time. No matter what time of the day you stopped in, you could almost always find someone you knew in there. Ashton Lane, and all the other cobbled lanes around Byres Road, had the feeling of a village set apart from the rest of the city in those days, and the café felt like a world set apart from the buying and selling that was going on elsewhere. The layout was very simple: two rows of booths with an aisle down the middle and the kitchen at the end. The seats were red PVC, the tables were etched with graffiti and there was a rumour that the owner, Larry, kept a gun beneath the counter.

Mark Jones was something of an incongruous presence in the usually downbeat and subdued café. He sat with his arms outstretched, his voice ringing out above the sounds of cutlery and quiet conversation as he told us all why Rhode Island were the best band in the world, and why we had to sign to his label.

We were bemused by his enthusiasm. We hadn't even played a gig together yet—Stuart had only met Isobel and Chris a couple of weeks beforehand—but Mark was already convinced of our brilliance and mapping out a future for us.

132

He told us that the label hadn't signed anyone to a recording contract yet. They were managing a band called Polar Bear, a three-piece from Northern Ireland, who were currently based in Dundee, but he wanted Rhode Island to be the first band on his label. He said he had the financial backing of a friend who worked on the stock market to get the label going, and said there were no limits to how far he could take us.

We were spread out across two booths, unable to fit round just one table—mainly because Mark had stretched himself out across one whole PVC bench to give himself ample room for his expansive hand and arm gestures. And he raised his voice again to make sure none of us missed his next point.

'You can make an album as good as *Hunky Dory*,' he told us. 'Stuart's songs are as good as Paul Simon's. As good as Dylan's. Rhode Island will be the next Radiohead. No question.'

He didn't make any secret of the fact that he didn't like the name Belle and Sebastian. Rhode Island had been the name written on the demo tape he'd heard, and he spent a while trying to convince us that we should stick with that, because it was less 'gay'. Then, when he realised he wasn't getting anywhere—and he seemed to have exhausted his reservoir of praise for the time being—he switched to talking about his own life for a while.

He told us that, when he was 15—and legally still a minor—his Dad had asked him to take the responsibility for some business problem his dad had got into, because Mark was too young to be prosecuted for it, and his Dad didn't want to risk having to go to jail.

133

'He's a great guy, my dad,' Mark said. 'I used to live with a girl called Jo, and I'd been going out with her for about six months before my dad finally met her. We went out with my dad for dinner and I introduced her. "*This* is Jo?" my dad said. "How *can* it be?" I asked him what he meant and he said, "I thought the Jo you kept talking about was a guy. I've told everyone you're gay." Great guy, my dad. Really great guy.'

He was subdued for a few minutes, while the waitress took away the remains of our lunch and brought us a dessert menu. Mark had told us his record company was paying, so we ordered The Grosvenor's legendary brownies and ice cream. After a few mouthfuls of brownie, Mark was back in high spirits again, his arms back up in the air, waving about furiously—and he was shouting, 'Anything you want. A-NY-THING you want! I'll give you anything you want to sign to my label. Just name your price, but you have to sign with me, guys. You have to.'

His voice rose to such a pitch I began to wonder if the fabled gun might make an appearance, dragged out from beneath the counter to encourage him to calm down. The staff turned to watch him in amusement. Then Chris, putting his empty plate aside, decided to step up to the challenge—and went first in naming his price.

'A pair of seventeen-inch flares,' he said. 'Plus, a date with Kate Moss and Celtic to win the Scottish Cup.'

And Mark promised him all three things, and looked around for the next series of requests.

There had been some debate about where in the flat the

gig should take place. We'd considered playing on the landing halfway up the stairs, and letting the audience watch from the downstairs hallway. We'd also considered clearing the furniture out of the kitchen and setting up in front of the windows there. But, by a strange coincidence, on the day after the party someone new was due to move into the mysterious eighth room in the flat, the room that had remained unoccupied all this time—and in preparation for their arrival a cleaner had come in on the morning of the party and left the door of the room unlocked. We decided that was the perfect venue for our performance; we pushed the bed up against the far wall so's some of the audience could sit there, and I set up the personal stereo speakers and a microphone in front of the windows, along with my bass amp and the ornamental bongos.

Arlene's enthusiasm for the party had remained undiminished. By the time it was due to start she'd invited most of the city, and when we raised the possibility of it turning into an uncontainable riot she had told us not to worry, she'd also invited the security team from The Garage nightclub. The ones who weren't working that night were going to come early on, and the rest would come when The Garage closed, as backup. It was alarming to realise Arlene considered this to be necessary, but also reassuring to know they'd be there. The fact that The Garage didn't close until four in the morning indicated that she was planning for the party to go all the way—and it certainly seemed set up to test the terms of the lease to their limit. Bringing in your own security team to deal with the carnage you were expecting definitely seemed at the far end of the spectrum from 'no overnight guests'. We braced ourselves.

First to arrive were the people who shared Wee Eric's house further up the street. Not all of them came, but there were enough to immediately fill the kitchen. It seemed that would probably have been a successful enough party as it was.

I talked for a while to a French girl called Babeth, who I'd seen storming around the games room up there but had never spoken to before. She wasn't happy to be at the party, badgered by Arlene into coming against her will, but she resolved to stay and see the band playing, then go home after that.

People continued to filter in, and most of them had a slight air of being there against their will, as a result of Arlene's strong-arming. But Arlene herself was on top of the world. She went from person to person, refilling their glasses and talking ten to the dozen, refilling her own glass almost at the same rate as she refilled the guests'—and for about half an hour she was on cloud nine, floating around like Beverley in *Abigail's Party*, while the doorbell rang and strangers continued to arrive. Then, quite suddenly, she disappeared.

I was talking to another friend from Wee Eric's house at the time, a girl called Vrnda who did Tarot card readings for us. And while we were talking Eric came across and told Vrnda that Arlene was asking for her. He said Arlene was in her room, so we followed him up there—and it was clear she hadn't asked us up there to continue her role as the perfect host and party person. She was unable to speak, ghostly white and vomiting into the sink in her room. A small crowd stood around her, which Eric now joined, holding her hair while she was sick and whispering to her reassuringly each time she straightened up.

'Close the door,' she said painfully.

Eric asked everyone except Vrnda to leave, and he locked the door behind us as we went back downstairs. I went into the kitchen and waited for Vrnda to come down. When she did she told me Arlene was in bed, already asleep. A little while later Eric reappeared and whispered that the party was over for Arlene.

'She always does this,' he said. 'Starts too fast.'

And then the guests really began to arrive.

Iain made free use of the two security guys who were already there, pointing out people he suspected were on the verge of doing some damage and asking the security guys to throw them out. Now that Arlene was fast asleep, we had no real way to tell who had been invited to the party and who had just followed the crowd and invited themselves. But Iain set about trying to find people he was sure had just gatecrashed the thing and pointed them out to the security guys too. Not that it affected the numbers by much; the rooms continued to fill up to bursting. And by the time we decided it was time to play the show, we had to fight our way into the room where we'd set up our equipment, and then push and scratch our way to the area we'd set aside for ourselves in front of the windows.

Arlene was already in bed by the time Stuart and Stevie arrived, so there was no longer any structure to when things should happen. We were all just guests in this chaos Arlene had created, and it was only the constant requests of Mark from Jeepster that finally got us started. Chris was working that night, and it wasn't clear if Isobel would be able to make it or not. She was playing a recital somewhere and had told Stuart she would come if there was still time. Stuart was trying to hold out in case she made it, but finally Mark's persistence—and the ever-present threat of the whole thing erupting into violence—won out, and we started up with just the four of us: Richard, Stevie, Stuart and me.

It was a very different affair from the only other house gig we'd played, in Alistair's front room. There were no programmes laid out on neat rows of chairs this time. There were no chairs—just the bed pushed up against the wall, where Mark sat with his arm around Stuart's friend Ciara, and then a heaving mass of bodies being pushed ever closer towards us, then surging back again just when it seemed certain they would fall on top of us. It was a stark contrast to the emptiness and quiet that had been occupying the eighth room since we'd moved in, and it wasn't all that easy to adjust to.

We played the songs we'd been rehearsing for the album. Stevie and me played through practice amps, while Richard tapped the bongos and Stuart strummed his acoustic guitar without any amplification and sang through the personal stereo speakers that we'd propped up on the windowsill. Through the open door, which faced us, we could see the crowd struggling to get a view from out in the hall; there were people everywhere. And every few minutes, usually during the quiet part of a song, the doorbell would ring again—and then more people would pour into the hall, and the crowd in the room would surge towards us again, getting ever closer.

We played eight songs in all, and when we were halfway through, starting out on 'Expectations', the doorbell routine kicked in again. The crowd in the hallway jostled for position, the usual annoyance appeared on the faces in the doorway as they were pushed out of the best spots and they tried to re-establish themselves, pushing back and being pushed away again. And then, as we watched them, mainly concentrating on what we were playing, a large metal spike suddenly appeared above the heads of the crowd in the room, making its way towards us, parting the bodies in front of it until a large gap had opened up and the spike was free to travel the path towards our performance area. It was only then that we could see what the spike actually was, what it was attached to. It was protruding from the base of a cello, a cello which continued being passed over the heads of the people in the crowd, and behind it Isobel was following along, taking hold of it when it finally reached our makeshift stage and sitting down on the empty chair to get herself into position.

'Sorry I'm late,' she said, as we stopped the song. She quickly introduced herself to Stevie, Richard and me, did a bit of tuning up, and then we started the song from the beginning again, with Isobel playing along.

I'd never heard a cello being played in real life before. I was thrilled by its tone, and impressed by how effortlessly and authoritatively Isobel played it. It seemed like it was the easiest thing in the world to her, and although, like Chris, she'd instantly struck me as being incredibly young, when she played she seemed to take on a sudden maturity, thoroughly absorbed in her bowing and fingering, nothing existing for her any more except the cello.

The crowd quickly reformed again, filling the path Isobel's arrival had opened up and surging towards us like they'd done before, and between songs Isobel looked up and giggled nervously at the chaos she'd stumbled into. Then, during the songs, she became fully absorbed and focused on her playing, seeming no younger than the rest of us. Mark Jones shouted for songs from the Rhode Island demo that we didn't play, and when we had done four songs with Isobel the show was over.

Their job done, Stuart, Stevie and Isobel got out as quickly as they could. Mark left soon afterwards too. Only Richard and me, with no other home to go to, stayed amongst the carnage after the gig was over.

There was a point later on in the party, when I was sitting up on a work surface in the kitchen, looking across the room at Richard who was crouching down on the floor near the fridge. He gave me a smile that perfectly encapsulated the madness that was going on around us, and that perfectly expressed the situation we were caught up in—prisoners in our own home, watching something unfolding that Arlene had put together in her haphazard way and then left us to deal with. Richard was a bit drunk and a bit the worse for wear, and his grin made me laugh for ages.

I spent an hour or so sitting out in the hallway, on the floor with my back against the wall. There was so much noise it was pointless trying to talk to anyone— there wasn't even any music playing, just the sheer volume of so many people shouting to be heard. The number of bodies crammed into the hallway reminded me of Beatbox in the early days. Phil, who had played keyboards with Rhode Island at the 13th Note, and who had once been the bass player in The Diggers—the band David Semple and the two Pauls had signed to the Beatbox label and then lost to Creation—was sitting in one of the few chairs that Arlene had set about the place. He gave me a smile similar to Richard's, one which acknowledged there was no point in us trying to speak with things as they were, and which also said, 'I'm glad this is your place and not mine.' A few weeks later, Gillian would move out and Phil would move in, but for the moment he was safe.

I was glad I'd decided to lock my room before the party started. Only the mysterious eighth room had been left open, and it was full of people still. I tried to imagine the destruction if the bedrooms had all been left unlocked. I sat on for a while, until Vrnda and Babeth decided they'd had enough, and asked me to get their coats from my room. We fought past the bodies upstairs on the landing, and when we got inside it suddenly felt strange to have such space and order inside.

'I don't think this'll ever end,' I told Vrnda and Babeth, and they said I could come up to their house if I wanted. I thought about it for a minute, wondering how I would ever sleep here, then I decided to stay. I unlocked the door for Vrnda and Babeth to leave, and when they had gone I stayed in the room on my own and locked the door again. I put some earplugs in, put some music on, and—while the chaos still raged—I got into bed and went to sleep, copying Arlene and hoping it would all be gone in the morning.

I found out the next day that everyone else who lived in the flat had done the same thing. And one of them—maybe Rhonda, maybe Richard—had phoned the police to complain about the noise before turning in, which meant that after we'd all dozed off the police had turned up and cleared the place out. When I woke up in the morning, everything was peaceful and calm. I took my earplugs out expecting the worst, waiting to hear the sound of the party still raging, but it didn't come—so I got dressed and went downstairs to assess the damage.

It looked bad. I was amazed and relieved not to find any bodies still lying around, but the mess was unparalleled. There was broken glass and cigarette ash everywhere. Empty bottles and glasses full of cigarette butts covered every surface. The kitchen floor was sticky and wet, the toilets were terrifying. But worst of all was the room our new flatmate was moving into that afternoon. I went in initially to check my speakers and my amps, to make sure they'd survived. They had, but the room itself was a disaster. I heard Iain getting up, and together we set about trying to put it straight.

I found broken glass in the bed, glass and cigarette butts trampled into the carpet, the remains of a fire in the sink. The empty bottles we took out of the room filled three bin bags on their own. We swept and cleaned and hoovered, each completed task opening up a whole vista of new levels of destruction to be put right.

While we were working, Arlene and Rhonda got up, and after a bit they got started on the hall and the kitchen. Arlene was still groggy, but overall she seemed amused by what had happened to her the night before.

'I'm so embarrassed,' she kept saying, rubbing her nose with the palm of her hand. 'Was it good? Were the band good?'

They sat eating breakfast in the hallway because the kitchen was too far gone to contemplate. Then when they'd talked enough, they had a go at that.

I was just picking up the last of the broken glass I'd found on the windowsill of the eighth room when the front door opened. Nobody rang the bell or knocked on the door—there was just the sound of a key in the lock and then the door creaked open. It was a girl we'd never seen before. I came out into the hall and we all stood staring.

'I'm Lauren,' the girl said eventually. 'I'm moving in today?'

She put her suitcase down just inside the door, and Rhonda stepped forward to welcome her.

'We had a party last night,' Rhonda said quickly. 'The place is still in a mess.'

'We thought you weren't coming till this afternoon,' Arlene added. 'I'm Arlene.'

Lauren nodded.

'I've still got a bag in the car,' she said, 'I'll go and get it. I won't be long.'

Thankful for the opportunity, we rushed back into her room to make sure we'd finished the job. Rhonda and Arlene wiped a few more surfaces, and I found one final piece of broken glass lying beside the sink. I carried it into the kitchen and then we tried to imagine how things would have been if we'd slept in for another hour or two; we agreed it didn't bear thinking about.

When Lauren returned with her bag, even the kitchen wasn't looking too bad. It was clear there had been a party, but maybe just a party with everyone who lived there and a few friends. She moved her stuff quietly into her room and seemed happy with the set-up and the decor. After a while she closed the door and went to work on unpacking, and we congratulated each other on a job well done. We started making breakfast and a few minutes later Richard appeared in his pyjamas, looking approvingly round at the place and nodding.

'Good-o,' he said. 'Good-o.'

Everything right with the world, and a new day dawning.

14

We played one more gig before making our album for Electric Honey, this time as the full band, out in a proper venue. It was something the pupils at Stow had to do as part of their course; organise a live event for the band they had chosen to make their record, and they set us up with a show in Edinburgh, at a bar called Stone's, behind Princes Street.

I wrote a letter to my friend Karn, who lived in Edinburgh, inviting her to come. And along with the students from the course and a delegation from Jeepster Records, she made up the sum total of the paying public.

Promoting the show was part of the students' remit, and they travelled to Edinburgh during the day to put everything in order. The band got the bus from Glasgow about an hour and a half before the show was due to start, squeezing in amongst the tired commuters with our guitars and cello. Stuart and Chris got off the bus somewhere in the Edinburgh suburbs to borrow a keyboard from a friend of Stuart's dad, because Chris still didn't have a keyboard of his own.

When we found the venue, Alan Rankine was alarmed to hear Stuart and Chris weren't with us, and that we weren't sure when they'd arrive. But since the sole promotion for the gig seemed to be a blackboard that was still sitting inside the venue, while the students finished chalking their 'Live Music' and 'Free Tonight' messages onto it, and neither Jeepster nor Karn had turned up yet, there wasn't any pressing need to get the gig started.

It was hard to tell what the students had been doing all day. They claimed to have distributed flyers around various other bars and cafés in the area, but their efforts hadn't brought in a single person. They'd constructed a stage area at the side of the bar, and Richard was setting up his drums at the back of it, but the venue had such a strange layout that it meant the audience would have to stand along the bar to watch, unless they sat in the booths in the corner behind us, or in the big empty area off to the side.

Mark from Jeepster turned up before Stuart and Chris got there, and he was so excited he was spinning like a gyroscope. He'd brought the other two members of Jeepster with him: Vanessa—who ran the office and dealt with the press—and Stef, who financed the operation. If the news that Stuart and Chris were still to arrive hadn't calmed Mark down a bit, it's likely he might just have popped. He spent some time prodding Alan Rankine, trying to get Alan as hyped as he was and constantly looking for Alan to assure him that Belle

146

and Sebastian were as good as he thought they were; then he spent some time trying to get Alan to agree that the name of the band should really be Rhode Island. He only gave it up when Stuart and Chris finally arrived. They came in just as the Electric Honey students were taking their blackboard outside to sit it on the pavement, ten minutes after the show was due to have started.

It didn't matter too much that Stuart and Chris were late. The students had spent so much time decorating their blackboard they hadn't noticed the electrical circuits in the venue weren't powerful enough to run the PA and the amps at the same time. With the blackboard duties fulfilled, though, they turned their attention to getting the show started, and it became clear that none of the equipment was working.

We climbed down off the makeshift stage and went back to our seats in a booth near the bar, while a lot of frantic running from place to place began and Mark started vibrating at an even higher frequency. He spun around the bar like a top, asking everyone he bumped into what was wrong—mostly being told each time that nobody knew. Then he would then oscillate on towards the next person.

While we were sitting watching the drama unfold, Karn arrived on her own, and looked around at the no-gig and the frantic toing and froing in the mostly empty venue. I called her name as she headed for the bar and she came across to our booth and sat down.

'I saw your blackboard outside,' she said. 'I don't think I'd have found it otherwise.'

I introduced her to Chris and Richard, and we

watched the students struggling to get the PA up and working.

'I'm feeling a bit weird,' Karn said. 'I just started taking Prozac a few days ago.'

It seemed like it might have been a good move, to help get through the evening that was currently unfolding.

After a while, the students started getting somewhere with the electricity, and they asked Stuart to come and stand on the stage while they attempted a soundcheck. They positioned a microphone near the sound hole of his guitar and moved the vocal mic around until he was happy with the height, then they asked him to strum his guitar and speak into the mic.

He looked uncomfortable, but he did it—and the only thing we could hear was the sound as it naturally occurred. There was nothing coming out of the speakers. Stevie went onstage and fiddled with his own guitar amp; he wasn't getting any power either.

Stuart kept strumming quietly, and then Vanessa from Jeepster—who none of us had been properly introduced to yet—shouted, 'Do it acoustically, Stuart. The band don't matter.'

And she started to dance.

Stuart blushed and mumbled that he couldn't do it without the band, then there was a loud hum and everything suddenly burst into life. Stevie's guitar made a clanging crackle and the students and Jeepster cheered at the arrival of electricity, and the rest of us climbed onto the stage and began to play.

For a first gig, it went well. And it had a lot of the

148

elements that were to become characteristic of a Belle and Sebastian show for the next few years. It was informal and relaxed, with points where it seemed like a whole song might fall apart, teetering on the edge of disaster, only to come back together again at the very last minute.

Stuart continued to insist that the drums should take their cue from his acoustic guitar, just like he had done in the Beatbox recordings, and Richard had to adjust his tempo and his rhythms to follow whatever Stuart was doing at the time. It made for some pretty erratic moments, but the combination of Stevie's virtuoso guitar playing with the strength of Stuart's songs, along with the compelling character of Stuart's voice, usually kept everything coherent; leaving the rest of us free to flounder around looking for the beat and the key, like a looser, drunker and infinitely quieter version of The Faces.

There was a lot of humour onstage between songs, and everyone in the band seemed to realise that it didn't matter if they made mistakes as long as the songs came across. We hadn't been together long enough not to make mistakes, and it was quite a liberating feeling. Suddenly, there was nothing to be nervous about—the worst thing you could do was hit a wrong note, and you were guaranteed to do that anyway—and the chances were that someone else would hit a worse one at the same time and you'd get away with it.

I spent a while sitting down on the stage, because things were so relaxed, and noticed another feature that was to become the norm for a while afterwards too: the reaction of the audience. Their enthusiasm seemed quite out of proportion to anything we were doing onstage. We were loose and shambolic and feeling our way through songs we hardly knew, yet the audience couldn't have been happier. Mark Jones and Vanessa screamed between songs, the students danced and sang along, even the barman stopped and watched. There were fewer people in the venue than there had been at our gig in the flat, but they made twice as much noise.

The songs we played were the songs we were about to record, and when we finished Mark started spinning around the crowd again, asking everyone if it was the best thing they'd ever seen, seeking reassurance that everyone loved the band as much as he did. Meanwhile the students did what they could to dismantle the equipment and the stage—because the show had overrun its time slot and the staff wanted to get us out as quickly as they could.

We tried to help, but Mark was intent on introducing everyone in the band—especially Stuart—to Stef and Vanessa, and beyond putting our instruments in their cases, his enthusiasm and persistence made it hard for us to do much else. I was keen to introduce Stuart to Karn too. They'd never met before, but their shared love of The Pastels, and the fact that they were the two people who had introduced me to indie music, made me think they'd get on.

'Come and meet Karn,' I said to Stuart, as he struggled to get some cables under control.

'Mark's hassling me to come and meet Vanessa,' he said.

I told him Karn was better, but Mark was soon beside us, pushing Vanessa towards Stuart, and as she launched into a critique of how great the show had been, I spent some time talking to Stef instead.

In comparison to Mark, Stef was very laid-back and attentive; he spoke quietly and thoughtfully and he dressed expensively, but stylishly too. He said he was happy to stay behind the scenes at Jeepster—just supplying the money and leaving Mark in full control of finding and promoting the bands.

Meeting Stef was something of a revelation for me. Growing up at the sharp-end of Thatcher's obscene reign in the 1980s, I'd naturally acquired the idea that all stock market traders were beyond the pale; that it wasn't in fact possible to be rich and humane. Mark had told us beforehand that Stef was a millionaire, and that he'd made all his money in the City, buying and selling stocks and bonds. I'd been expecting the worst—I'd never met a millionaire before. But Stef seemed like a perfectly lovely guy; a bit shy, but quick and astute, in full possession of all the more subtle social skills that Mark consciously eschewed.

If Stef could be such a decent guy, I thought, even though he was a millionaire who had made his money from something other than music, art or literature, then maybe my assumptions had been wrong. Maybe it was possible to be both a rich businessman and a passable human being.

When it came my own turn to meet Vanessa, I found out she had worked with Momus in the past. Before moving to Jeepster, she'd been working for the publisher of Momus' songs, and she said she knew him quite well. I tried to keep her on that subject, but Mark was only interested in talking about Belle and

Sebastian—and while Vanessa enthused about what an exceptional talent Stuart was, Mark explained to me how everything would be fine when the band were making Stuart's songs sound more like Radiohead.

'Make sure this album sounds like *The Bends*,' he told me—then one of the bar staff mercifully shouted to us to start moving out of the venue. I tried to shift the conversation back onto Momus, and somehow, before Vanessa disappeared, she had given me a phone number and an address where I could contact Momus if I wanted.

I imagined Semple's face when I showed that to him at Beatbox.

Karn walked back to the bus station with us, and I finally introduced her to Stuart on the way. The Electric Honey students, along with Mark and Stef, Vanessa and Alan Rankine, had vanished into the night as soon as we left the venue, and we walked along the dark, empty streets in a scattered group, at our own pace, enjoying the normality again after the hyped-up atmosphere of Stone's Bar. I told Karn we should meet up again soon, and we talked for a while about how bright the stars were, then she left us to catch a taxi home.

The bus we climbed onto was deserted, and we spread ourselves out on there, taking all the window seats and putting our instruments down on the empty seats beside us. As we crossed the country back to Glasgow I studied the stars again, and felt happy to be part of the band, happy to be living with the people I was living with at the flat and happy to have seen Karn again.

I began looking forward to making the album,

feeling amazed at what had just happened to us. We'd only played two shows together as a band, one at home and one in public that the public hadn't bothered to come and see. I'd only met Chris and Isobel a few weeks earlier, and yet we were about to make an album together. And Jeepster wanted to sign us up to make another one as soon as that was finished. It was all a bit bewildering. There were bands at Beatbox, bands at The Halt Bar, who had been together for years, who had gigged relentlessly—who had managers and merchandise and good word of mouth—and nothing had happened for them. And here we were as if by magic…

PART THREE

Tigermilk

15

We started making the album for Electric Honey on Monday 4 March, 1996. We had three twelve-hour days for the recording, 10 a.m. to 10 p.m. Monday till Wednesday, then Thursday and Friday to do the mixing. And the biggest thrill of all was that we were recording in Cava Studios, the most hallowed studio in Scotland at the time.

Sitting on the edge of Kelvingrove Park, Cava was based in an old church, with a domed roof and Greek-style columns at the original entrance. It looked very grand, and it was. Most of our favourite Scottish bands had recorded albums there, and the live room was awe-inspiring. Retaining the original structure of the church, it was a long, broad, curving space that ran all the way up towards the domed roof, with a full-size grand piano at one end of the room and an enclosed drum booth at the other. There were TV rooms upstairs with leather armchairs for when you weren't working, and at the top of the stairs, a door led into the original body of the church, with its pews and its balcony—which had been left unreconstructed, and was sometimes used for filming court scenes in the TV drama *Taggart*.

But what really made our jaws drop was the studio's control room. In comparison to the control room at Beatbox it looked like the flight room of a spaceship. The room itself was huge, but the mixing desk filled it quite easily, stretching off into the distance—a retreating landscape of sliders and glowing buttons. It was surrounded by acres of built-in effects units, and there was a separate room off to the side housing the tape machines, with their huge reels of unbelievably wide tape. Another little room stood apart for recording vocals, and above the huge window that looked out into the live room, built into the wall, were two of the biggest speakers we'd ever seen.

Chris began to giggle uncontrollably as Gregor, the in-house recording engineer, showed us round—and it was clear that we'd crossed the threshold into another world.

Stuart had often spoken to me about his plan for how he wanted the drums to sound on the album. The drum sound was key to getting the vintage quality he was after.

'Just two overhead mics,' he kept saying. 'The way they recorded drums in the sixties.'

That had been his approach when we'd recorded in Beatbox too. Engineers always loved mic'ing up the drums—close mic'ing each piece of the kit individually, using as many mics as their arsenal allowed, sometimes putting two mics on the snare drum alone.

'We won't be doing it like that in Cava,' Stuart had told me. 'No way.'

But once we'd been given our tour of the place, and Gregor had introduced us to his assistant and tape op, Geoff, they let us set up our equipment in the live room. And while we were doing that, Gregor and Geoff huddled around Richard, and as soon as his drums were in place they broke out their weaponry and got to work on wiring him up to the moon.

Geoff dashed back and forward across the live room, grabbing mic stands from wherever he could find them, arranging a vast network of them in Richard's booth, while Gregor said things like 'The AKG or the Fifty Seven?' and clipped long leads onto the mics he was fixing to the stands.

Stuart nudged me while I was tuning up my bass, and he stood watching them in horror.

'I think they're mic'ing up the whole kit,' he said. 'They are, aren't they? They're mic'ing up the whole kit.'

He tried to persuade me to go and tell them we only wanted a stereo pair above the kit, but I was too shy.

'You tell them,' I said, and he grimaced, breathing in sharply.

'Maybe it'll be OK,' he said, looking completely unconvinced.

'You should just go and tell them,' I said, brave enough with my advice for something I knew I couldn't do myself.

'I'll let them finish what they're doing,' Stuart said. 'Then when we listen to it I'll tell them if I don't like how it sounds.'

159

Gregor and Geoff continued building their megalithic construction, and Stuart stood watching them, agonised. Then eventually he said, 'I'm going to do it,' and he wandered off towards the drum booth.

As soon as he reminded Gregor that he only wanted to use two mics on the drums, overhead, rather than mic'ing the whole thing up, Gregor told Geoff to start dismantling things again—and he was perfectly friendly about it all. It was the first time we'd had such an amiable response from an engineer, and suddenly it felt as if everything was going to be all right. Gregor instantly made us feel that we had every right to be there, that our opinions were perfectly valid, and all the years of being given bad mixes by amateur engineers, of being told we were wrong for thinking it should be otherwise, just melted away.

When Stuart had insisted it wouldn't be a problem for us to record the album in three days, he hadn't quite factored in that it would take us most of the first morning to set up, and for Gregor and Geoff to mic the amps, arrange the isolation booths and baffle boards and organise a monitor mix in the headphones that everyone was happy with. It was almost lunchtime before we made an attempt to put anything on tape, and when we finally did the results were far from encouraging.

We started out with 'The State I Am In' and 'Expectations', just instrumental versions without Stuart singing. Although we were nervous—and there were a few false starts and clanging errors that brought proceedings to an abrupt halt—we'd rehearsed enough to know the structure of the songs well, and we soon

160

had a couple of takes that had gone smoothly enough to be worth listening to.

We climbed the stairs into the control room brimming with excitement. So far we'd never heard a recording of ourselves, and with the standard of the equipment that was being used, the vintage microphones and all the banks of compressors and effects units, all running into the hallowed desk to be perfectly EQ'd and balanced, we were expecting to hear ourselves transformed. We gathered together on the sofa at the back wall of the control room, hushed and expectant, while the tape decks clunked and whirred in the faraway room. Then Gregor turned on the huge speakers and started the tapes playing. There was a brief silence while he pushed a few buttons and moved a few faders up and down, then the opening bars of 'The State I Am In' rang out.

And it sounded terrible.

It wasn't just that we didn't sound as good as we'd hoped we would, or that we'd raised our expectations too high and it was something of an anticlimax. It actually sounded genuinely awful. Muddy, flat, lifeless and sloppy. There was no singing, and for a long stretch at the beginning it was just Stuart's acoustic guitar, my bass and Richard's drums. It sounded worse than anything we'd ever recorded in Beatbox. Much worse, even, than the recordings we'd made in my attic on the four-track machine. And suddenly it felt as if we couldn't possibly make an album. Not in a year, and certainly not in the two and a half days we had left.

Stuart asked Gregor to stop the tape, before it had gone very far, and I asked him why it was booming so much. He looked around the desk for a minute, then said he'd try it through the monitor speakers instead of the huge cabinets built into the wall, in case we weren't used to them yet. The tapes whirred and clunked again, back to the start, and although I prepared myself for the worst, this time it didn't sound so bad. It was still lifeless and flat, but it didn't sound like it was coming from an underground cave any more.

'We're going to have to play to the singing,' Stuart said. 'All together in the room, without the baffle boards and the isolation.'

'It'll be difficult to keep the instruments from bleeding into each other if we do that,' Gregor said, but Stuart shrugged.

'Let's try it,' he said, and we slouched back to the live room again with a lot less wind in our sails than we'd had to begin with.

Gradually, things started to come together. The huge wall speakers had been too big a leap for us after the personal stereo speakers we'd been using at home, but as long as we confined our listening to the smaller monitors, and once we had a mix where Stevie's guitar sat properly in place like a glue holding all the other instruments together, things started shaping up.

Because we were recording onto tape, and because multi-track tape was so expensive, we couldn't afford to keep alternative takes of each song. Nowadays, recording onto hard disk, it's normal to keep dozens of takes of each song and decide later which one is best. But using tape, on the tight budget Electric Honey provided, we had to decide as we went, to free up tape

162

for recording the next song. We sometimes managed to get three takes of a song without any disastrous mistakes, then we would go and listen to them through. And although there were usually still overdubs to be done, scratch vocals to be replaced and proper mixes to be applied to the drums and guitars, we'd have to choose there and then which two versions to discard and which one to keep, so's we could move on.

It was Stuart's job to make the final decisions, and he didn't always choose the take which was the best technically. He'd often go for one where the timing was shaky, or where someone had hit a clanging chord that wouldn't be easy to remove in the mixing process, because its echoes had bled into the mics of the other instruments. But he'd choose the one he liked based on how alive it felt, or how apt an interpretation of the song he thought it was, often to Stevie or Richard's dismay. And then Gregor would roll the tape towards the beginning of a take he'd rejected and pause, with his finger on the transport control.

'You're sure?' he'd say. 'That's definitely the one you want to keep?'

And Stuart would nod slowly, while the tape machine would start up again, and Stevie or Richard would let out a sigh as the recordings with fewer mistakes or steadier beats disappeared for ever.

The students from Electric Honey arrived en masse during the first afternoon of the recording. Part of their remit was to fulfil an A&R role during the sessions, to give them experience of yet another aspect of the music business. And although we didn't know it at the time, never having had any experience of A&R ourselves, they did a perfect impression of the real thing. They set up camp in the control room without any ceremony, talking loudly amongst themselves, then asked to be played what we'd recorded so far and immediately began offering unflattering opinions about it and making suggestions for how we could improve what we'd done to make it sound right. It went on for about half an hour, until Stuart quietly asked Alan if he could take them away and not bring them back. It was blatantly clear that we couldn't get any work done with them there—and although they were supposed to come in for a similar session every afternoon, and to play an active role in the mixing of the record, Alan accepted the fact that it would only upset things to have them come back again.

In retrospect, he probably realised that being banned from the studio while the record was being made was as real an A&R experience as they could have, one that would prepare them for any proper A&R job they might acquire in the future. And no doubt he also realised that Belle and Sebastian had now also felt the full force of the A&R experience, which we learned from immediately—and applied the same blanket ban to all future A&R requests to visit the studio while recording was in progress.

*

Things slowly began to take shape over the next couple of days. Once we'd accepted that the quality of the equipment in Cava, compared to anything we'd used

164

before, only exposed our flaws rather than making us sound better than we were—and once it became clear that Stuart wasn't looking for perfection anyway—the same air of relaxation that had surfaced at the Edinburgh gig began to assert itself again, and we started to enjoy the process. As the finished takes stacked up they gave us the dizzying sense that we were actually pulling it off, we were really making an album and the feeling that had accompanied the first playback of 'The State I Am In'—that it had been crazy to even think it could be done in three days—began to evaporate. A particular character began to emerge in the takes we were keeping, a particular dynamic began to surface in the way we were playing together and a particular mood began to permeate the sessions as a whole. It wasn't just the album that was coming together, it was Belle and Sebastian as a band. We started to get a feel for what we could do as a unit, for what kind of a unit we were.

Although we'd only fallen together six weeks before—had only played one proper gig as a six-piece—and had only really communicated through Stuart previously, mainly rehearsing with him individually, the fact of being thrown together for the intense experience of recording in Cava, and spending twelve hours a day together in there, had suddenly forged us into a gang. Quite by luck, or by Stuart's intuition in putting us together, it transpired some kind of special chemistry was emerging—a slightly shambolic magic. And it was being caught on tape. Captured at the instant it was being born.

It wasn't until we had live takes of all the songs that

guests started coming in to do overdubs, and add the colour and texture to the bare bones we'd recorded. Mick Cooke came in to play trumpet, Joe Togher played violin, Kenneth Hume played flute. We were into the days set aside for mixing by then, and Gregor and Stuart mixed as they went, getting the rest of the band to do drop-ins on the worst mistakes we'd made as they came to light.

Stuart had most of the arrangements for the songs already worked out before we started recording, and he'd hum the guests' parts to them while Gregor was mic'ing their instrument and sorting out their mix, gradually piecing together the orchestration he'd been carrying around in his head since the day the song was written. But there were times when things just occurred to him when we were listening to playbacks too. The relaxed and spontaneous atmosphere carried on through the mixing and the overdubbing. If anyone came up with an idea there was always time to try it. Stevie often heard a second guitar part that he'd go in and play—and sometimes it worked and sometimes it didn't. There was no real restriction on the number of overdubs we could add to a song, like there had been on the number of takes we could keep of a backing track. There were forty-eight tracks available on each song— not unlimited like with hard-disk recording, but still way more than were needed.

One evening, when the guest instrumentalists had all gone for the day, Stuart decided he wanted to put the sound of a music box on the start of 'Mary Jo'— something that sounded like an ice-cream van in the distance. He'd brought in a gadget with a tiny handle

166

that turned a metal drum against a row of pitched metal strips, and he realised that when it was sitting on the glass coffee table in the control room it sounded much louder than it normally did. The body of the table was amplifying it. So Gregor decided to mic it up right there in the control room, to get the best sound he could from it. He spent a while positioning the mic, keeping Stuart kneeling on the floor turning the handle continuously while he checked the signal in his headphones. Then when he was happy, he let the sound come through the monitors and EQ'd it for a while, adding reverb and adjusting its depth and length until he had what sounded like a convincing ice-cream van.

The whole process had taken about twenty minutes by the time he was finished, which was quite a chunk of time compared to what had been spent on a lot of the more central work we'd done so far. But it was a fun diversion, and Gregor asked Stuart if he was ready to go for a take and rewound the tape to the start of 'Mary Jo'.

Stuart stood up and stretched his legs, stiff from all that kneeling while Gregor was setting up the sound, then he flexed his fingers as if he was a concert pianist about to perform a tricky recital and knelt back down in front of the glass table again. Gregor put a finger to his lips, indicating to those of us sitting on the sofa against the back wall to stay quiet while the tapes were rolling, and he hit record. The acoustic guitar began to play and Stuart nodded along—then, just at the point where he thought it should be, he focused his attention, grabbed the little handle between his thumb and index finger and began to turn.

There was a moment of confusion, and then the control room erupted into laughter. After all the work, after all the mic'ing and tweaking and waiting, the music box turned out to be in entirely the wrong key for the song. It sounded like a hellish cacophony. Dropping his head, Stuart picked up the music box, put it in his pocket, and Gregor stopped the tape.

*

Although the students from Stow had been banned from attending any further sessions, there was a steady stream of friends of the band coming and going, particularly as we got into the mixing process. A couple of Moondials dropped by, Richard and me brought flatmates in for a visit, Stuart's friends Ciara and Joanne came along, as did a few strays from Beatbox. It was exciting introducing people to this new world we'd been allowed to inhabit for a week, and we'd loved being there ourselves. We'd grown accustomed to the place. Chris, Bel and me in particular started to wonder how we'd function when it was all over, dumped back into the dull world, without Gregor, without Geoff, and without the constant supply of freezing cold water in cone-shaped paper cups from the water cooler at the bottom of the stairs, which we'd invested with an almost mystical significance.

On the second last day, while we sat waiting for Gregor in the control room, Joanne—who had come in for a look at the place—suddenly burst out laughing.

Stuart was sitting near the mixing desk with his acoustic guitar on his knee, and he asked her what she was laughing at.

'What?' he said. 'What is it?'

But she just shook her head, and then she laughed again.

'What's so funny?' Stuart said, and Joanne pointed vaguely towards the mixing desk, then swept her hand around to encompass the whole studio.

'All this,' she said. 'I'm thinking of you sitting in the kitchen in the flat, with that little tape recorder. And now, all this.'

Stuart smiled and nodded quietly.

'It's brilliant, isn't it?' he said.

'It's unbelievable,' Joanne replied.

She looked around at everything again, and for a moment I felt envious of Stuart. I'd always thought I would be working with my own band in studios like this by now, recording my own songs—but it hadn't happened. Stuart had believed it would happen for him too, and now here was one of his friends confirming that it had. There was no doubting that everything had come together for Stuart at that moment; he'd hit his songwriting stride, he'd found some of the people he wanted to play on his songs, and he had the interest of the industry—enough interest to let him put his vision into action. Somehow, I was no longer writing complete songs, no longer had a band, and was quite aware watching Stuart arranging and mixing his songs with conviction that, for the moment at least, I'd lost the singularity of vision to pull that off for myself. It was a long way from the future I'd dreamt for myself as a teenager, but as Gregor returned to the control room and started up the mix of 'We Rule The School' again,

I realised I was happy.

Something quite unexpected had taken place during the five days we'd spent together in Cava. We'd started the week as a loose collection of people who were helping Stuart to make his record, but something quite special had happened and we'd emerged at the end of it as a band. An unusual and awkward band—a strange collection of people from different backgrounds, of different ages, with different aims, but all outsiders of one kind or another—and I felt glad to have somehow ended up amongst them, to have made something with them that seemed worthwhile.

At the end of the last day we had a play-through of everything in its finished state, and Stuart, Chris and Bel got up to dance behind the mixing desk during the playback of 'I Could Be Dreaming'. They all had their own dancing styles. Chris was Northern-Soul-Boy, Bel School-Disco, with her pigtails and white knee socks. Stuart was somewhere between Punk and gym hall jogging.

It was joyful to watch, a shy celebration of what we'd achieved, but there was a bittersweet quality to it too—everyone knowing that our tenure at Cava was over. We'd packed our instruments away, all the microphones and patch leads had been dismantled and the live room had been tidied up and prepared for whoever was coming in next. All the mixes had been bounced down onto two-inch tape, and when the playback was over there was nothing much left to do except say our sad farewells to Gregor and Geoff and then go home.

Chris, Bel and me also had our respects to pay to the water-cooler at the bottom of the stairs, the symbol for

170

us of everything that had been great about the week. Then, with that done, Chris said to me, 'This has been the best week of my life. But I'm not sure if it's just because I've had a shite life up till now or not.'

He disappeared up the stairs, while I went back along the corridor to pick up my bass, and before I got outside a rumour had begun to circulate that Chris was crying.

A knot of people stood at the door, band and studio staff, chatting in the darkness, and as I stepped outside I saw Chris standing amongst them. He came towards me with his eyes still red and said, 'I think I embarrassed myself earlier.'

I asked him if he had cried, and he screwed up his face.

'Maybe,' he said.

'You're gorgeous,' I told him, and then we all went home.

16

It was strange to be back in Beatbox again on Monday morning, after the time we'd spent in Cava. Both places did have a lack of daylight in common, but that was where the similarities ended. The control room of the Beatbox studio seemed very small and cramped now, the equipment inadequate and dated. And more pronounced than anything else was the lack of purpose and structure to the day. It was back to sitting around in the corridor knowing nothing would happen, and it was very difficult to adjust to after the sense of direction and the order we'd had making the album.

Everyone in the band had gone back to something similar. Richard was back in the classroom at Stow College, taking lessons along with the students he'd been able to ban from the studio a few days earlier. Chris was at uni through the day, studying for his physics degree and washing dishes in a restaurant at night to pay his way. Bel was in Jordanhill College, working on her music degree, serving drinks in a piano bar to tired businessmen in the evenings. And Stevie, determined to uphold his decision not to join the band, had got himself a job driving the minibus at a care home in Erskine.

With Stuart, I was back in Beatbox, and the only thing I had going on for the time being was an evolving narrative with David Semple, based on the fact that I was carrying Momus' contact details around with me. By that point David was being referred to as Dr Semple, because he was constantly quoting the Momus song 'Trust Me, I'm a Doctor' whenever anyone questioned the validity of his opinions on anything. But just recently Momus had become embroiled in a tabloid scandal, appearing on the front page of the *Daily Record*. He'd married a seventeen-year-old Bangladeshi girl whose parents had forbidden her to see him, and now they were threatening Momus' safety. Momus and the girl had escaped to Paris, and were in hiding at a secret location. But Dr Semple maintained that, because I was carrying Momus' contact details around with me, I was in constant danger.

It wasn't much of a diversion, but, along with a band rehearsal at the weekend for a gig we were about to do at the Art School, it got me through the long empty weeks following the making of the album.

The Art School gig, on Wednesday 20 March 1996, stood in stark contrast to the show we'd played at Stone's in Edinburgh a few weeks earlier. Whereas that audience had consisted of the Stow students, my friend Karn and an out-of-proportion reaction from Mark Jones and Vanessa from Jeepster, the crowd gathered at the Art School while we were waiting to go onstage seemed very real, very large, and quite intimidating. There were journalists from the *NME* and *The Scotsman* there to write reviews; A&R scouts from London record companies had come to find out if the hype they'd heard about us—probably from Alan Rankine and Mark—was justified, and then there was the Art School audience themselves: hip, cool and not easily impressed.

It wasn't just the crowd that was different though; we were different now too. We knew each other, we felt like a band rather than just a bunch of people who all knew Stuart individually, and we'd found something of an identity—a sound and a style—since we'd last played a show.

Still, we'd never played this size of gig before. In all the time I'd been playing with Stuart, this was looking like it would be the most important gig we'd played. The show at The 13th Note had had a smattering of the kind of audience Stuart wanted to play to, the gig in the flat had had the numbers and at Stone's there had been some industry people—but here they were all rolled into one. Suddenly it wasn't pretend any more.

We sat out in the crowd watching the support act, at a table next to a pillar that separated the gig area from the pool tables. The pillar was wide, with an alcove built into it, and Stuart was sitting up in the alcove hugging his knees to his chest. When the support finished he closed his eyes and I felt grateful for a moment not to be in his position. He looked nervous, and although I was free of the nerves that had always overcome me before going onstage when I was younger, I knew that if I'd been upfront leading the band—playing for this audience—I'd have been nervous too.

'Are you all right?' Bel asked Stuart, touching his shoulder.

Stuart nodded and kept his eyes closed.

'I'm focusing,' he said.

Then he climbed down from the alcove and we all made our way to the stage.

The stage in the Art School wasn't too different from the stage in Stone's, a raised platform about a foot in height tucked over in the corner on the opposite side of the room from the bar. There were areas off amongst the pool tables where you couldn't see the stage for the alcove pillars, and another big seated area at the far end of the bar where the walls hid the stage completely. But a packed crowd formed in the area directly in front of the stage, and we started to play.

Quickly, though, it became obvious that the usual glue that held everything together was missing from the mix; we couldn't hear Stevie's guitar. There was some crackling and a loud buzz, but that was all, and as the first song ended the soundman came onto the stage and started hunting around for the source of the problem. He didn't stay on the stage for long. The moment he discovered what it was he leapt back out onto the dance floor as nimbly as a cat, and then told the rest of us to put our instruments down and get off the stage, all except for Richard. He told Richard to continue sitting at the drums, without moving and without touching anything.

Richard put his arms out to the sides, as if he was balancing on a high wire, and looked from side to side. Then he turned very pale when the soundman told him

175

what the problem was: the foot of his drum stool had cut through the power cable of Stevie's guitar amp, and the drum stool itself had become live.

We all stepped further away from the stage and the soundman instructed Richard to get up very slowly and very cautiously—making sure he didn't touch any metal parts of the stool as he got up. That was only the beginning of his ordeal, though. Once he was on his feet the soundman persuaded him that he was the person best placed to break the circuit, by uncoupling his drum stool from the live wire of Stevie's cable, since he was already on the stage anyway. Richard didn't seem convinced, but the soundman insisted, so—reluctantly—Richard agreed to do the heroic deed.

From a safe distance, and in a less than reassuring tone, the soundman told Richard there was nothing to be frightened of as long as he followed the instructions.

'Just grab the stool by the seat,' he said. 'But very slowly, and be careful not to touch the legs.'

Richard looked round to see if there was another option, maybe wondering if he could just dodge out the door at the side of the stage and go home, then he bent forward and put a hand on either side of the padded seat.

Nothing happened.

'All right,' the soundman shouted. 'Now, very slowly—very slowly—lift the stool clear. Just take your time, and then put it down over there.'

Richard stared at the cable where it had been split by the foot of his stool, where the bare wires were still touching the foot that had cut them, then he eased it up and away, up till the seat was level almost with his chest—then he moved off to the side, putting the stool down with much more haste than he had lifted it, and he hopped off onto the dance floor to a round of applause from the crowd.

The soundman was brave enough to climb onstage then and turn Stevie's amp off at the wall. With that done he quickly repaired the break in the cable, and then, disaster averted, we reassembled on the cramped stage and started the gig again.

This time, it went OK.

*

When Stuart decided to move out of the flat on Sauchiehall Street, I asked Diane if the landlord she worked for had any more vacant rooms. She found Stuart one on Hillhead Street, up near the university, but he didn't stay there long. The guy in the room next to his was an Iron Maiden fan, and he played his music loud—so loud that Stuart didn't get much peace.

'It's a good flat,' he told me. 'Just bad luck.'

He wrote 'Mary Jo', watching a woman in the flat across the road, imagining her life. Then he moved out.

'Something else will turn up,' he said. 'I'm leaving it to fate.'

And something did turn up.

Just when it looked like he was about to become homeless, the minister at his church in Hyndland told him the caretaker was retiring, and he offered the caretaker's flat to Stuart, as long as he was willing to take on the caretaker's duties. All at once, Stuart had a whole flat to himself, a job of sorts and a place to

177

rehearse and write songs when there was a break between the various youth clubs and coffee mornings that took place there.

The church hall looked unassuming from the outside, like a school gym hall built onto an old brick building as an extension. But inside, it was Tardis-like, with doorways and corridors stretching off into far distant corners. From the front door a staircase twisted up into the flat, and to the left were two more doors, one leading into the church hall itself and one into the meeting room and kitchens—a sort of backstage area for church people.

In the daytime the church hall was always flooded with light, a luminous place. It was long and wide, with high windows running lengthways along the walls, and the wooden floor, the wooden walls, all seemed to soak up and reflect the light at the same time, bathing everything in a warm, welcoming glow. And, perhaps more importantly for us, it didn't just visually glow in there; it glowed acoustically too. Every sound reverberated around the same wooden surfaces, and became coated in the same honey-rich tones as the light.

Stuart loved the sound of the piano in the church hall. He loved the sound of his acoustic guitar in there too. And because he wanted to hear everything coated with that same golden echo, we began to rehearse in there. We rehearsed without microphones, with amplifiers turned down low, with Richard using brushes instead of sticks on the drums—so that the volume didn't override the echo, so that the sound of the hall almost became a member of the band itself. And when

178

we'd practised with it to a point where we didn't quite sound the same anywhere else, Stuart decided to bring an audience into the hall, so they could hear us in what had become our natural environment.

The audience was mainly family and friends, but now that we'd made an album there were a lot of family and a lot of friends who were curious to see what all the fuss was about, so it was a good-sized crowd.

Food and drinks were laid out in the meeting room, where everyone gathered for a while before the show. In some ways it was the mirror image of the Art School gig. There, the audience had been cool and aloof, the atmosphere charged and excited, the room itself shadowy and dark. Here the atmosphere was warm and friendly, the audience (some of whom had been at the Art School too) open and unguarded, and the rooms were full of light and fresh air.

With our instruments lying in wait on the stage in the hall, we introduced friends to friends, family to family and indulged in the food and drink ourselves.

Stuart was half in his role of bandleader and half in his role of church hall caretaker. When it was time for the show to begin he ushered the crowd out into the seated area in front of the stage, hurrying the stragglers along and making sure no one took any food through to the hall.

I was talking to Stuart's friend Ciara, and she asked me a question that I didn't know the answer to while Stuart tried to move everyone on.

'You're very mysterious, Stuart David,' she said.

Stuart stopped beside us.

'Who is?' he asked.

'He is,' Ciara said, pointing at me.

'Stuart David?' Stuart said, and shook his head, 'No he's not,' and he guided Ciara into the hall towards a seat.

There was one major difference between the stage in the church hall and all the other stages we had played on before—it was high. Very high. We looked down on the rows of foldaway chairs as if we were a school band playing in the assembly hall. The fact that it was still daylight added to that feeling too, but the sound was great. We played to the volume of the hall, and the hall magnified us and supported us with its echo.

The relaxed attitude we'd found onstage at Stone's was amplified too. Playing in front of friends and family there was no pressure anyway—but it was another step in moulding the irreverent way we played together, and in accepting that mistakes were going to be inevitable and weren't the end of the world. At one point, Chris hit a chord that was so fantastically wrong, so devastatingly awful, that he collapsed in a fit of giggles and couldn't play on. We continued, with his laughter reverberating and being given as much amplification by the hall as the music, and a lot of the audience joined in too. There was a gap before the next song to let everyone gather themselves together, and then we started up again.

Soon, the audience had picked up on the idea that we weren't taking anything too seriously, and they began to play along. They started to act the part of a stereotypical pop audience—the girls screaming, the older people clapping in time, and by the end of the show most people were up out of their seats and dancing.

'We should do all our shows here,' Stuart said when we were clearing up afterwards. 'I wish everyone could hear the way we sound in the church hall.'

In a way, it had been like a much bigger version of our gig in Alistair's basement flat, inviting a group of people into the environment where we'd been practising, inviting them into the place where we knew we would be at our best. There were twice as many people in the band now, the room and the audience were much bigger too—but the idea of controlling the environment was the same. At the Art School we'd struggled with the standard PA and the bad acoustics of the room—we'd played for the audience we wanted to play for, but not in the way we wanted to play. It seemed that in trying to take what we were doing out into the world to let people hear it, it often became something other than what we wanted them to hear.

The aim was to try and bring them into our world, as it was.

17

When I first started writing to my friend Karn, she was at art school in Dundee, sharing a house with one of my friends from school, James Cameron. One day James sent me a letter, telling me that he thought I would like Karn, and inside his letter there was a letter from her too.

So we started writing to each other. We met up now and again, but mostly we wrote—and just after the show at the church hall we realised we'd been writing for almost seven years. It seemed like a long time to us, so we decided to meet up to celebrate the occasion—in the real world.

In our letters we'd often spoken about beaches—wild beaches, deserted beaches, beaches where the waves were high and austere—not the holiday beaches of sunshine and sand. So we decided that, for our anniversary, we would go to a beach.

Shyly, we met up in Glasgow and caught a train to Gourock, and from there we took the ferry to Dunoon.

It wasn't a warm day. We sat on a bench at the ferry terminal, looking out over the grey water, hoping it wouldn't rain. Karn told me about her ex-boyfriend Alan, how he'd recently been in touch because he wanted to get back together. They'd arranged to meet up, then—at the last minute—he'd cancelled, saying he'd been to the zoo with the girlfriend he'd just split up with, and he was in love with her again.

We walked out to the edge of the pier and looked down into the water, leaning on the railing. The water was calm and deep and grey. We watched the ferry coming into the terminus, and got ready to board.

As we sailed across to Dunoon I told Karn about the shows we'd just played at the Art School and at the church hall. And I told her that I thought the album was going to sound good when it came out. Stuart and Stevie had taken the two-inch tape down to London on the train to be mastered, and Stuart said he'd felt the same way he'd read Morrissey and Johnny Marr felt, taking the tapes of 'Hand In Glove' down to London for mastering—as if they were in possession of something secret and special, unbeknownst to all the other passengers on the train.

But the album still didn't have a name. Stuart was working on the cover artwork and the tracklisting, and he didn't want to name it until that was ready.

I told Karn about all that stuff, and she told me how Prozac was really beginning to help her. In the past, we'd always struggled to talk much when we met up, but as we stood out on the deck of the ferry and watched the seagulls swooping in and out of the trails the ferry was leaving, we seemed to be doing OK.

Things seemed to be flowing.

We caught a bus from where the ferry dropped us off near the centre of the town, and rode it round the peninsula to what we'd heard was a good beach. We didn't have any real plan for what we were going to do when we got there, but in my last letter I'd finished with a P.S. that said, 'And if you want, you can take my bony hand along the shore.'

That seemed like a bit of a plan.

The beach we found was broad and long and deserted, with dark-coloured sand stretching off towards the distant firth, miles away at low tide. We climbed over a wall and walked across the dry sand until we reached the line left by the high tide, kicking about amongst the driftwood and feathers and seashells and litter before we carried on across the wet sand uncovered by the retreating tide.

Halfway to the sea, Karn said, 'I had the strangest dream last night. There was a puzzle in it I was trying to solve—like a crossword puzzle, but without the words.'

She picked up a stick and started drawing the puzzle in the sand: a huge square divided into four smaller squares by drawing a cross inside, then the smaller squares were all divided into smaller unequal sections, some with patterns inside, some without.

'It kept feeling like I was just about to solve it,' she said. 'But now I can't remember what it was all about.'

'Maybe we can work it out now,' I said, but she shook her head—so instead we decorated the framework using debris from the tideline, filling in the squares using shells and twigs and feathers and old tin cans, making a collage from the structure of her dream.

When it was finished we walked down to the edge of the water, and stood with the waves lapping up to touch the toes of our shoes. The wind was cold, and there wasn't much to look at out there, so after a while we turned round and started walking back up the beach again. There was a large white house in the distance, separated from the beach by the main road, and it had a single towering tree in its garden. A fir tree, seeming to reach up into the sky—and we talked about it as we walked; how it should have been on a mountain somewhere, maybe in the Alps, with snow dusting the branches at its peak; how it seemed bigger than the house itself.

When we reached the picture we had made on the beach from Karn's dream I asked her if she wanted to take my hand, like I'd said in the P.S. in my letter.

'Take it where?' she asked. Then she held her hand out and told me it was very cold.

We walked back to the road holding hands, still occasionally talking about the tree in the garden next to the white house, and once we'd crossed the tideline and the dry sand we stepped over the low wall back onto the pavement and walked towards the bus stop. Halfway there, a lamp post appeared between us and we passed it one on either side, holding our arms out behind us until the lamp post wouldn't let us go on further until we separated our hands.

When we wrote to each other about the day afterwards, we both agreed that we seemed to have beaten our difficulty of talking to each other in person the way we did in letters. The first time we met up, when we'd only been writing for a few months, we'd spent seven or eight hours together wandering around the city and we'd hardly spoken a word, we were too shy to talk at all. But afterwards, we'd written easily about how the day had been for us both, and that pattern had continued every time we'd met up after that. The silences had become like a curse, one that we didn't seem to be able to break. But this time, something had changed.

We wrote about the crowded bus we'd caught back into town, and the owl we'd seen chained to a perch in a garden we'd driven past. We wrote about the fun we'd had in an arcade playing the penny falls, and about the group of children who'd watched us while we were winning big, shouting –

'That guy! That guy!' while I was bending down to scoop my winnings out of the hole low down on the machine, and –

'That wummin! That wummin!' while Karn was crouching down to pocket hers.

And we wrote about how much we'd both enjoyed the day, and how easily we'd talked on the train back to the city, and we agreed to meet up to do it all again sometime soon.

*

As part of their course, the students at Stow College had to take part in an exchange visit with students on a similar course in France. In May, with their band chosen and their record made, they went off to spend a week attending the French college—and part of their work there involved arranging and promoting a show for their band to come over and play.

And so, with Richard already in France working on the project, the rest of us—Stuart, Stevie, Chris, Bel and me—travelled to Ramsgate and took the ferry across the Channel to join him.

It was a rough crossing, not like the one I'd made to Dunoon with Karn. The waves were high and the ferry rose and fell with them, dropping off the crests into the troughs with a horrible thud. We were queasy and disoriented by the time we landed, but there wasn't really any time to find our equilibrium again. We were met at the terminus on the French side by one of the local students from the French college, and he piled us all into his car with our instruments and our suitcases—then he asked us, in what seemed to be the only English he knew,

'You like to Rock? Yes?'

And although we told him we only really liked to rock a little bit, he nodded and told us,

'I like to Rock! Yes!'

And he cranked his stereo up full, blaring Def Leppard and shaking his long blond hair across his face as he drove, thumping the palms of his hands on the steering wheel in time to the beat.

It was something of an omen for the show to come.

When we left home we'd been under the impression that as well as hotel accommodation and our meals being provided, we'd also be getting per diems to cover our expenses while we were in France. I don't know where the idea had come from, but we'd come to believe in it as being fact by the time Rock Boy dropped us off at our accommodation. As it turned out, it wasn't only the idea of our expenses that had been a misunderstanding. There were no meals being provided either, and our accommodation was in an old woman's guest house, where there were only three beds, flowered wallpaper and the overpowering aroma of mothballs. None of us had brought money with us—we didn't have any to bring—and now that our metabolisms had recovered from the violent ferry ride and the alarming driving of the French student, we were starving.

'I'm sure we can eat with the kids from Stow,' Stuart said. So we dropped our bags and instruments off at the guest house and went out to try and find them.

It wasn't easy, but we eventually found Alan Rankine sitting with a few of them in a bar near the college. Alan had just finished eating a pub dinner, and at first he seemed pleased to see us.

'How was the trip?' he asked. 'How are you all?'

'Starving,' we replied.

At that point we were still expecting we'd be getting food from somewhere, but Alan told us that wasn't part of the deal.

'You'll have to buy your own,' he told us.

'We haven't got any money,' we explained, and he asked us why we'd come to France without any money.

'Because we haven't got any,' I said.

We told him we'd been under the impression our meals were being provided as part of the trip, but he shook his head.

'That's just the students,' he said. 'They eat in the college canteen.'

It was quite late by then, and it had been a very long

day. We'd travelled hundreds of miles, and the thought of having to get through the evening and all the next day without any food, and then do a show at night, was pretty overwhelming.

'Can you buy us something to eat?' I asked Alan, but he told me he didn't have any money either.

'You must have some,' I said. 'We could pay you back later.'

It wasn't an easy ride, and I think in the end we had to say we wouldn't be able to play the show if we didn't have any food. Eventually, Alan bought a few dishes at the bar for us to share, and said if we turned up at the college canteen tomorrow lunchtime he would try to sort out something for us there.

Then, still hungry, we wandered back to our guest house—and tried to work out where we were all going to sleep.

In the final arrangement, I had to share a bed with Stuart, in a room decorated with flowered curtains and pre-war furniture, like a museum installation set up to evoke life in the early 1930s. Stevie and Chris shared a similar room, while Bel—hitting the jackpot—got one to herself.

When I woke in the morning Stuart had disappeared. I took full advantage of having the bed to myself, stretched out and slept on, and it wasn't until I had finished getting washed and dressed that Stuart turned up again. He'd been out for a run and had written a new song in his head while he was jogging through the characterless town. He picked up the guitar and stood by the window working out the chords for it.

'What do you think of this?' he asked me, and started

singing a verse which began with a line about jazz boys and jazz girls.

The tune was perfect. It twisted and turned towards a point where it seemed as if it was just about to take off for a soaring chorus, then it stopped.

'That's all I've got so far,' Stuart said.

I told him I loved it. It seemed to me perfectly simple and perfectly alive, and I envied the ease with which he'd come by it, and the effortless way the words, melody and chord sequence all hung together. I had the feeling that if I could do anything, this was what I'd like to be able to do. Write as effortlessly and perfectly as that.

'It still needs another section,' he said, and put his guitar down. And it must have been that the other section didn't arrive, because I never heard the song again.

When the band were collected together, we set out to walk to the college where the students were taking part in their exchange, to see if we could qualify for lunch in the canteen. Richard and Neil met us there, and it turned out they were operating on a voucher system. At the beginning of the week, when they arrived, they'd all been given a bunch of blue paper tokens, and each one entitled them to a meal in the canteen while they were studying in the college. Neil rounded up some of the Stow students and tried to get them to donate a coupon or two each to our cause. They weren't keen on the idea.

'We'll have nothing to eat by the end of the week,' one of them said.

'I'll sort it out before then,' Neil told them. 'I'll talk to the tutors.'

They weren't convinced he'd be successful, but—reluctantly—they handed over a few of their tickets to him. We couldn't drum up enough for a lunch each, but we put what we had together and made a sharing buffet. Then we sat at the Formica tables, looking out over the blank docklands, wondering if the show would be good enough to make the trip worthwhile.

The venue, a nightclub in the centre of town, was huge inside. It was long and narrow, slightly S-shaped, with the stage at one end and a balcony at the other. Two narrow extensions of the balcony ran halfway down the long walls towards the stage, and various doors led off into other bars and lounges.

We turned up early, halfway through the afternoon, having nothing better to do. We dumped our instruments in one of the dressing rooms, upstairs near the balcony, and hung about until someone came along to help us soundcheck.

In twos and threes the students from Stow began to arrive in their capacity as promoters and organisers of the gig. They stood around watching, much as they had done at Stone's in Edinburgh, their numbers slowly growing while Richard hit the drums one thump at a time and the sound guy stood at the mixing desk, halfway down the hall, twiddling knobs and moving faders. When Richard was finished, the rest of us had a shot at going up on stage alone and playing solo while the sound guy fixed more levels, then we all played together for a song or two, while he balanced the mix for the whole band. It wasn't a very successful soundcheck. The guy was intent on giving us the standard rock mix, and whenever Stuart asked for any adjustments the sound guy invoked the language barrier to disregard his requests. It was the polar opposite of our sound in the church hall—we were right back in the days of being lost in an environment of someone else's making, attempting to take something out into the world that became something other than we intended just by taking it out there.

Neil and a few other students made slight but unsuccessful attempts at mediating between the band and the sound guy, then the support band—a local outfit called Loch Ness—turned up to do their own soundcheck, and we accepted that we'd done all we could do and relinquished the stage.

Things didn't look hopeful for the gig, but just as we were packing our instruments away and carrying them back to the dressing room, Alan arrived at the venue and announced he'd treat us to dinner before the show, much to our relief.

Despite the fact that their name was a cosy reminder of home, Loch Ness turned out to be a complete mismatch with our band. Probably chosen solely on the Scottish associations of their name, they took to the stage as if they were already rock stars stepping out in front of a stadium crowd. The place was packed by then, and we stood up on the balcony looking down on the enthusiastic audience, deafened by the interminable thrashing of Loch Ness and the wild cheering that erupted on the rare occasions that one of their songs came to an end. Because we were sharing amps with them, it was clear from their mix that our soundcheck had been a waste of time, and the only consolation we could take while we stood upstairs was that, since they were the support band, their set should be mercifully short.

It should have been, but it wasn't. In the end, they played for over two hours. We waited for it to end, and we asked some of the students from Stow to try and sort it out after the first hour had passed. They made attempts at trying to convince the sound guy to call time, and at trying to talk their fellow French students who knew the band into pulling the plug, but none of it came to anything. It was clear by then that the crowd were Loch Ness's crowd, friends and family they'd brought along to make sure the gig was their gig, and even when it looked like it was over, it wasn't. They played four encores, and then—sometime after midnight—they disappeared out of the venue and the whole audience went with them, leaving us facing the same people we'd faced at Stone's in Edinburgh—the Stow students and Alan Rankine—in the cavernous and empty venue, without even Karn to make up the numbers.

The show was a sorry affair. The venue looked so empty and so vast that it didn't even seem as if all the Stow students had stayed. Alan sat at a table halfway down the hall, slouching in his chair next to the tutor who ran the French music business course, and we played our set through squalls of feedback, struggling to reclaim our earlier mix from the adjustments Loch Ness had made during their set.

At one point, I completely forgot the chord sequence for 'I Could Be Dreaming' and went so far off the rails I had to stop playing for a while and just mime. Later, Stuart got so frustrated with the pointlessness of the show that he took his guitar off and made a misguided attempt at stage-diving. It wasn't successful. He only really succeeded in bumping into a couple of people who were standing near the front, then stumbling over onto the floor. After that, he climbed half-heartedly back onto the stage and we carried on.

The one bright spot in the show was when we played the cover version we'd been keeping up our sleeves, a song we'd practised a few times at home but hadn't played at the soundcheck. A slow, piano ballad version of 'Party Fears Two'—Alan's biggest hit with The Associates. He seemed genuinely surprised, and genuinely moved—and we played it with affection and admiration. There were rumours that he'd shed a few tears during the performance, but we decided to believe that was more to do with the disastrous outcome of the trip rather than anything else.

There were no Loch Ness-style encores for us. We finished amidst a smattering of applause and a wail of feedback, then we unceremoniously began packing up our gear without even leaving the stage. And when that was done, we headed back to the guest house for one more night stranded in the 1930s.

*

Even the trip home was disastrous. It began with the same guy who had picked us up at the ferry driving us

194

back there again—with Guns N' Roses full blast on the car stereo this time, telling us, 'I remembered—you like to Rock! Yes!'

Exhausted and hungry after having played a truly pointless show, it was even less endearing than it had been on our arrival—and it cemented my feelings about 'Rock' from that moment on. Rock had never been something I cared for before, but my feelings had been un-crystallised, a loosely gathered collection of irritations and ideological intuitions. Now, I had a single point of reference to throw them all into sharp relief— and my rejection of 'Rock' was complete.

The trip to the ferry was only a rehearsal in miniature for the full ordeal of the trip back to Glasgow, though. When we were crossing the Channel we came to the realisation that, on top of all the other organisational shortcomings of the trip, we hadn't actually been provided with any means of getting home. Our train tickets only went as far as London, and when we got there we were stranded—without food and without money.

It was Jeepster who eventually came to our rescue. After some hunting around in pockets and suitcases, we came up with enough spare change between us to call Mark Jones from a phone box, and he directed us to the Jeepster offices. From there, we were fed and entertained, and provided with train tickets home.

We'd already missed the last train by then, so the people from Jeepster gave us beds for the night. I stayed at Vanessa's with Chris and Bel, who danced to Vanessa's records until after midnight—then we slept until just before 5 a.m., when we had to get up again to catch the train.

We'd been saved from the incompetence of one record label by the kindness of another—and there was no longer any doubt about who we'd be signing to for the future.

18

The Equi café was second only to The Grosvenor in our affections. High up on Sauchiehall Street, almost at Charing Cross, it hadn't changed its decor since the late 1970s. The walls were lined with fake wood panelling, and the seats were upholstered in brown PVC. It was very dark inside, and there was one booth in its own alcove at the back of the café that we always tried to commandeer. It usually wasn't difficult. Most of the time, the café was close to empty, with one old lady sitting at the table in the window, while a couple of teenagers bunking off school huddled up against the far wall.

The booth in the alcove was almost its own café, set apart. The table and the alcove walls were covered in intricate graffiti, and even the low ceiling had its fair share of ink carvings etched into the fake wood.

The menu was unreconstructed from the 1950s— fried egg rolls and bacon sandwiches, pots of tar-like tea and thick pea and ham soup.

Stuart had started going there while he was living just a few doors down in the flat shared by Joanne and her friend Helena. In the mornings, walking to Beatbox, he often left the keys for Joanne with the woman behind the counter because they only had one set between them. He wrote about that in 'String Bean Jean'.

I'd been going there since before I moved to Glasgow, on Saturday afternoons with my friends Dougie and Gordon. But now that I was only a street away it became my favourite place for band meetings.

One afternoon, while Stuart was finishing off the cover for the album, we all met up in The Equi to go over something he wanted to talk about. The booth was empty, so all six of us wedged ourselves in and waited for the pots of tea to arrive.

For a long time, Stuart had been certain about the running order of the album. The sequence of songs he'd written up on the whiteboard at Stow, when he was trying to convince Alan we could make an album rather than a single, had remained almost constant from conception through recording to mastering. But now he was considering a radical change.

'I think I'm going to start the album with "I Could Be Dreaming",' he said. 'I've been listening to it sequenced like that. I think it works.'

It was a surprise to everyone. His thinking all along had been that the quiet beginning of 'The State I Am In' would draw people in—that the intimacy of it would set the tone for what was to come. It was going to be a calling card for the band, a first introduction to the world that was also a statement of intent. Initially, it had taken some of the band a while to come round to the idea, but now his announcement was met by a questioning silence.

The waitress arrived then and clattered cups and mugs down on the table, itemising the orders as she went to make sure she'd got everything right. We fixed her mistakes when she'd gone, swapping cups and cutlery until everything was the way it was supposed to be. Then, as the commotion died down, tea was poured and the statement Stuart had made rose up in the silence again.

'I don't think you should do it,' I told him, but no one else made any comment. The silence continued, broken only by the sound of cups touching saucers and the woman at the counter rearranging her display.

I wasn't sure if what I'd said was the right thing to say or not. In some ways, I was just presenting Stuart's earlier argument back to him—restating something that he'd convinced us all of in the first place.

'I think it would be a better opening,' he told me, and still nobody else said anything.

For some reason, at that point in time, I thought he was wrong—and it became a conviction.

'I think it would ruin the album,' I said, and Stuart looked surprised. 'It's up to you,' I told him. 'But I think it'll be a weaker record opening with "I Could Be Dreaming".'

I knew it was Stuart's vision, and I was wary I might be missing something and potentially ruining a better structure that I couldn't see. I think everyone else felt the same, which is probably why they hadn't made any comment. We were all used to how certain Stuart was in his convictions by then—and we were all aware of the fact that it was his band, his record, and that only he could really know what he was trying to achieve. But I stuck to my position.

'I'll think about it again,' Stuart said. 'I'll have another listen.'

And we changed the subject to other things.

*

Stuart was well into the writing of *If You're Feeling Sinister*—the second Belle and Sebastian album—even before the first one was released. While he was working on the artwork for the first record—and while we were rehearsing for the shows at the Art School and the church hall—he was impatient to move onto rehearsing for the next one.

'I can't wait until all the songs are written,' he said to me one day in Beatbox. 'I can't wait until it's time to hand out the folders of lyric sheets to everyone in the church hall.'

At the time, that particular ambition made me feel uncomfortable. I wasn't sure I wanted to be sitting in the church hall being handed a folder of songs, as if I was a pupil in Stuart's imaginary classroom, while he played the teacher. We'd already been briefly introduced to a couple of the songs, though, and they sounded great.

One afternoon we'd had a band rehearsal in my room at the flat, and Stuart had given us a run-through of 'The Stars of Track and Field'. It took a couple of listens to grasp that the structure of the chorus based more on dynamic changes than harmonic ones, but once we'd got the hang of that it was thrilling to play—not quite like any other songs we'd played so far. Stevie stayed behind for a while after everyone else had left, and he couldn't stop talking about the new song.

'It gives me that feeling,' he said. 'I love it.'

We tried to play through it a few more times ourselves, remembering what we could, feeling our way. And as I tidied up the chairs and cups the band had left behind, and Stevie talked some more about how much he loved the tune, it felt as if the initial awkwardness between us was being laid to rest.

*

The day of handing out the folders finally came. There were only five songs to begin with—half the album. Stuart had decided to concentrate on completing the first batch of songs so's we could get started on rehearsing, and to continue working on the other five until they were fully realised.

The folders were A4 size, pink cardboard, with each song inside printed on a single sheet of A4 paper. Once Stuart had handed each of us our folders he gave us all a pen too, and then we went through the songs one by one, noting the chord changes above the lyrics in whatever style suited us. It was, as I'd expected, like being in a classroom where Stuart was the teacher—but it was clear that the songs were even stronger than they had been on the first album.

'The Stars of Track and Field' was amongst the first batch of songs, so was 'Like Dylan in the Movies'. Stuart had already written a bass part he wanted me to play on that song, and when we'd noted down all the chord changes on the sheets in our folder, he showed it to me. Then we began to rehearse the songs. We rehearsed them every Sunday afternoon in the church hall until the five songs were completed, with the sun flooding in through the high windows and the acoustics enhancing everything we played. It was like being in a world unconnected to the business world that was beginning to intrude into what we were doing—a world that was delicate and unpretentious and pure.

*

Even before we signed to Jeepster, Mark Jones started looking for an American label he could license our second album to, to help fund its recording and promotion. His idea was that, although Jeepster didn't have a lot of money themselves (despite his earlier claims that they'd give us 'anything we wanted' to sign with them), they could do a deal with a big American label to release the record everywhere outside of Europe—and the American company would pay an advance which Jeepster would split fifty-fifty with the band. It didn't seem to matter to Mark that we hadn't formally agreed to sign with him yet, he thought his idea was a winner, and he went all out to make it happen.

He got results too. By the time of the launch party for the Electric Honey album he seemed to have stirred up a feeding frenzy amongst some of the biggest label bosses in the world, and on the evening before the party he flew up to see us with Seymour Stein, the head of

Sire Records—the man who had signed Madonna and had given The Smiths their American record deal.

Mark booked them into One Devonshire Gardens, a large converted townhouse on the corner of Great Western Road and Hyndland Road, and the place where Michael Jackson and U2 stayed when they were playing stadium shows in the city. It had a five-star restaurant, priceless old masters on the walls and an eclectic collection of antiques furnishing the rooms and the hallway. Mark had arranged for us to meet them there early in the evening, and so—without Stevie, who was still working at his job in Erskine—the five of us walked up Hyndland Road after meeting in the church hall and stood outside in the garden shouting, 'Jonesy!' up at the bay window until Mark's sheepish face popped up above the windowsill.

A minor kerfuffle then ensued, a doorman coming out into the garden to see what all the fuss was about and attempting to move us on and away from the exclusive residence. Then Mark appeared behind him and explained that everything was OK.

'They're with us,' he said, and the doorman frowned disapprovingly. The doorman remained on the steps for a few more minutes, wondering if he could keep us out just by blocking the entrance—then he gave up and Mark told us to come inside.

The hotel was surprisingly small inside, and Seymour Stein was sitting in the bay window of the lounge, which wasn't much bigger than a normal-sized living room. Every detail had been calculated to convey the hotel's exclusivity and expensiveness, though, and fresh from the poverty of Beatbox, from our rented rooms in shared flats and from our recent run-in with the doorman, it all rubbed us up the wrong way. The other guests, scattered sparsely around the room, watched us closely. Conversations stopped, wine glasses were lowered, we became the centre of attention. We were certainly making more noise than anyone else in there, teasing Mark for the opulent surroundings he'd chosen for himself and voicing our disbelief at finding ourselves amongst them. But what was really getting most people talking was Chris's coat, and as we sat down at Seymour Stein's table, Seymour himself couldn't take his eyes off it.

'Woah,' he said. 'That's quite a statement.'

The coat in question was fake fur, long and dark brown, an unreconstructed 1970s original, probably a woman's. To add to the effect Chris was also wearing a pair of denim flares with fifteen-inch bottoms, but the impact of the coat was so strong the trousers were going largely unnoticed.

'You know,' Seymour said to Chris, 'you remind me of Johnny Marr in that thing. That's the kind of coat Johnny used to wear.'

Chris began to giggle uncontrollably, more flattered than he could endure, and made no reply—so Seymour started talking to Stuart instead.

There was something in Seymour's appearance that made him look utterly debauched. He was like a Roman emperor, one from the tail-end of the empire who had indulged in too much of everything, and the surroundings of One Devonshire Gardens suited him perfectly. There were deep purple swellings beneath his eyes, he was fat in a regal way, and it wasn't too difficult to imagine him with a crown of laurel leaves encircling his bald head.

He spoke in a high-pitched voice, with a soft and lazy quality, and when it became clear that the guests were only becoming more impatient the longer we stayed, he suggested we should go round to the church hall so that Stuart could play him some songs.

'Would that work?' he asked, standing up. And although Stuart hadn't had any prior warning that he was going to have to perform, the decision was made. Mark ran upstairs for his coat; then, in a ragged group, we made our way down Hyndland Road in the sunshine, much to the relief of the doorman and the rest of the guests at the hotel.

There was no living room in the flat above the church hall, just a big open-plan kitchen, with a wooden floor Stuart had painted pale blue. We settled in there with Mark and Seymour—standing around the room or sitting on the floor.

Stuart wasn't keen to play without the band; he began by saying that he couldn't do it. But Mark kept coaxing for 'just a couple of songs', done acoustically, since Seymour had flown all the way from San Francisco to meet us, and couldn't stay for our performance at the launch party the next night. We'd been under the impression that Seymour was only going to be treating us to dinner—there hadn't been any mention of playing for him—and there were echoes of Vanessa's shout in Stone's Bar that the band didn't matter in Mark's coaxing. But finally Stuart gave in to his requests, and went to get his acoustic guitar.

He played 'The State I Am In' and 'She's Losing It', standing with his back to the three tall windows. He wasn't comfortable doing it; it was clear that playing with the band making up most of his audience made him uneasy. But it was a good performance, and after the second song Seymour said excitedly,

'I'm sold. I'm pre-sold. Let's go eat.'

And we called for some taxis to take us to an Indian restaurant where Mark had already booked a table.

None of us had been in the restaurant before, but it was vast. It had a domed ceiling and a balcony area, and we were seated at a long table right in the middle of the room, a table so long it was impossible to speak to the people at the other end.

Neil from the Stow College course met us there too, in his role as Mark's A&R man for Scotland, and because there were so many of us Seymour started ordering one of everything on the menu, deciding we would just lay it all out in the middle of the table and share whatever we wanted.

The amount of food that eventually arrived was unbelievable. It was just like being at the kind of Roman banquet Seymour's appearance had initially suggested: decadent, rich and plentiful. Mark encouraged us to take as much as we could eat, attempting to give the impression that this was the world he was used to, that this was where he lived day to day. Seymour himself didn't have any conception of another world. For him, this was just how things were—irrefutably.

I sat at one end of the table, with Chris, Bel and Neil. Far away from us at the other end, Stuart was sitting isolated between Mark and Seymour. He seemed to be miles away, almost in another country, and we couldn't hear any of their conversation. Mostly we ate, for a long time; when one course had become boring, Seymour would order a whole raft of new dishes for the next one—and so it went on.

The message was quite clear; if we signed to Sire Records for America, this was the kind of plenty we would have access to. And Mark, by association, wanted us to believe that if we signed to Jeepster, this was what he could do for us. This was the 'anything you want' he had promised us in The Grosvenor Café. And as main course dishes followed starters, and cakes and desserts followed the main courses, there appeared to be no foreseeable end to it all.

'I don't think I want my life to be like this,' Isobel said at one point, and Chris agreed. Stuart started making cross-eyed faces at us from the far side of the table, whenever Mark and Seymour were occupied with something else—and by the time Seymour asked the waiter for the bill, three hours had passed. The restaurant was empty of other customers by then; waiters stood idly around the empty space, waiting for us to leave so's they could close the place up. When the bill arrived, we managed to catch a glimpse of it before Seymour took it under his control. The total cost of all the food we had eaten, or at least attempted to eat, was exactly twice my monthly income. I'd never seen a bill like that before—it looked like a roll of wallpaper. We were used to the little square of paper from The Grosvenor and The Equi Café, with two or three items scribbled in black pen—and a total that never reached double figures.

And then the crowning glory of the evening arrived—a huge silver platter over half a metre in diameter, its entire circumference laid out with After Eight mints, the rest of the plate heaped high in the centre with boiled sweets and jelly beans. Together, Neil and Chris counted two hundred After Eights, and then—since this offering was free—we crammed as many of them as we could into our jacket pockets.

Mark and Seymour insisted on calling for taxis to take us all wherever we wanted to go, while they were ordering their own car to take them back to One Devonshire Gardens, but we declined their offer. After such a long evening and after so much food, we were in need of some fresh air and a good dose of the reality of the Glasgow streets. We walked home together somewhat bewildered, in a kind of daze and an opulent fog, trying our best to become our impoverished selves again.

As it turned out, Seymour Stein decided not to sign us anyway. The fact that we had no plans to tour America in the next year or two, because Chris and Isobel would be beginning their final years at university after the summer, made him decide we weren't a commercially viable investment—but we did have a plentiful supply of After Eight mints for a long time to come.

19

Tigermilk was launched on the evening of 6 June 1996 with a party at Cava Studios, where we'd recorded the album four months earlier.

There had been no title for the album until Stuart finally settled on the photograph he wanted for the cover. It was a picture he'd taken himself, of Joanne in the bath, breastfeeding a toy tiger, and although Stuart had also become a fan of Tiger's Milk bars when he was in San Francisco, the title of the record was really just a descriptive term to accompany the photograph.

The cover became a major project for Stuart, and he worked on it with Andy Symington, the DJ at Glasgow's Northern Soul club Divine, who had perfected his Photoshop skills making flyers for his club night. For Stuart, the cover was almost as important as the songs on the record, certainly the main way for him to communicate the visual world the songs existed within, and it wasn't until he was completely satisfied with it that anyone at Electric Honey got to see it.

Although the album wasn't officially launched until 6 June, copies of it began to circulate a week or two before that, first as a white-label test pressing and then in the full cover. I got my own copy a week before the launch party, and because I didn't have a record player at the time I took it to my brother's flat to play it there. Afterwards, I wrote in a letter to Karn –

'I love it. I don't much like the first song on the second side—except in places. But I love the rest.'

And a couple of nights later Mark Radcliffe played 'The State I Am In' on Radio 1, saying the album had been made by some schoolkids on a course at a college in Glasgow. He played the track in full, explaining he'd received it in the post a few days earlier. When it ended he said he thought it sounded quite special—particularly since it had been made by schoolchildren.

Returning to Cava Studios for the launch party was a happy experience. In the afternoon we set up and soundchecked in the live room of Studio One, and it was like returning to a spiritual home we'd been evicted from on the day we finished recording; almost every door and staircase had a sentimental value attached to it.

We set up with our backs to the control room, facing out into the main area of the live room—all together in a way we hadn't been at any point during the recording. There was no stage, just some rugs laid out to designate the area of the floor that was ours, and we spread out amongst the pillars in that part of the room.

Strangely, the set we were going to play was mostly made up of the songs we'd been rehearsing for the new album. Although it was a launch party for *Tigermilk*, Stuart had already moved on from a lot of *Tigermilk*'s songs, and he didn't see any point in revisiting them. So the set we played was just a snapshot of the band as it was at that moment, three months after the album was recorded, rather than a live version of *Tigermilk*.

An hour before the party was due to start, we returned to the studio and the place had been decorated with hundreds of copies of the *Tigermilk* LP. They lined the walls of the staircase leading down to the live room, they sat on windowsills and furniture in the lounge upstairs, they stretched in a long line along the top of the picture rail that ran from the lounge to the kitchen. The students from Stow College had arranged the display after we'd finished soundchecking—and the albums were there to be freely taken by whoever wanted them, once we'd played our set.

It was a thrill to see so many album sleeves, all identical to each other, filling the studio in the way they did. It was like a Warhol exhibition where the multiples could be taken home. And to see our own album filling the place that had made such an impression on us when we were recording there was quite magical. It established a connection between us and the place that we hadn't been expecting.

It was more of a shock for Joanne, though, to see herself duplicated to infinity, and she shielded her eyes and hurried past as quickly as she could, both on the way in and on the way out.

The launch party was the Stow students' final assignment. Once that was over, they had completed their course—and learned as much about the music

211

business as they were going to learn. While we waited in the control room of the studio until it was time for us to play, Alan Rankine told us the students had done an admirable job in putting the launch together and they were expecting over three hundred people to be there—which was as many as the live room could hold.

He also reeled off a list of all the London record companies who were sending A&R to the show, and the length of it was overwhelming—Island Records, EMI, Sony Music, Virgin, Chrysalis… it went on and on. He made it sound as if the students had suddenly acquired incredible organisational skills in the weeks that had passed since the disaster that was the French trip, but it was clear that it was really Alan who had used his connections in the business to make sure the evening was a success.

'We're going to sign to Jeepster anyway,' Stuart told him, and Alan nodded slowly.

'Don't rush into anything,' he said. 'See what else is on offer,'

But Stuart wasn't interested.

When they opened the front doors we went down into the live room to look for people we knew. I met Isobel's parents and brother for the first time and introduced them to my own family. Her dad was a policeman, her brother a rugby player—and they were both no-nonsense guys in a way I hadn't expected. Most of the people we knew from Beatbox were there too—and most of the people from my flat. David Campbell was there, Stuart and Richard's parents—and in amongst them all, all the record company people and music

212

journalists Alan had told us about.

When the room was full, full almost to bursting, we assembled on the rugs and picked up our instruments. By then, the rugs were no longer exclusively our domain. The crowd had spilled onto the area designated as a stage. People leant up against the pillars and stood between members of the band. The front row were face to face with us, pushed up so close our noses were almost touching.

'All right?' Richard said, and Stuart nodded.

Then we started.

We began with Stuart at the piano for 'We Rule The School', and although the people were packed into the room like sardines, they were silent from the moment Stuart started singing. He hardly played at all on the opening lines, singing very gently, just brushing the keys now and again, and it was something of a first to hear such a crowded room so quiet. Then, one by one, the rest of the band joined Stuart's more deliberate playing until the silence disappeared and the room was full of music.

As things went on, the distinction between the band's area of the room and the audience's section became less and less clear. More people leant up against the pillars and stood between us; Chris, who was at the opposite side of the set-up from me, was far more distant than thirty other people who weren't in the band. When Isobel was sitting down to play cello I couldn't see her at all. But all through the set the audience remained quiet and attentive, only breaking their silence between songs to applaud.

Near the end, Stuart took the chance to thank all the

other people who had played on the album, and who had helped to make it in one way or another. Last on his list was Keith Jones, a fellow inmate from Beatbox.

'Is Keith here?' he asked, 'Keith Jones—where are you?'

Stuart put a hand on his brow, as if he was shielding his eyes from the sun and looking out to sea.

'Where's Keith?' he asked again, and people in the audience looked around to see if anyone was raising their hand.

In Beatbox, Keith was somewhat out of place. It wasn't clear if he liked music or not, and he certainly didn't look like most of the musicians on the course. He wore smart checked shirts, neatly pressed jeans, and with his short blond hair and decidedly functional glasses he could easily have been an escapee from a maths course at the university. He was young and he spoke very fast, and in some ways he was as incongruous in Beatbox as Dr Semple. They both seemed to belong somewhere else, but there was one difference between them—Keith did actually spend his time making music. He never had a day in the studio; he never wanted one—he didn't have a band and he didn't play in anyone else's band either. But most of the time he could be found in the computer room, sitting in front of an Atari ST, absorbed in Cubase. He'd become the resident expert on Cubase, always able to tell you how to do whatever you were stuck with, always willing to teach you a new procedure. But he never let anyone else hear the music he was making—it wasn't even clear that he was making music—his interest was strictly in *using* Cubase, exploring its possibilities, learning all of its features.

And then, one day, Stuart found out Keith had a synthesiser at home—a real analogue synthesiser from the 1970s. I'm not sure how he found out, but as soon as he knew about it he started trying to persuade Keith to bring it in.

'I can't believe you've got a Moog,' Stuart kept saying.

'It's not a Moog,' Keith kept replying, 'it's a Korg 700s.'

'You should bring it in,' Stuart told him. 'You have to bring it in, Keith.'

Eventually Keith surrendered.

Stuart had made two songs on Cubase—one called 'Sleep the Clock Around' and one called 'Electronic Renaissance'. Stuart didn't much like Cubase, but he realised he could make it sound a bit like New Order—which amused him—so he made those two songs. Then he managed to book a few hours in the studio to add his vocals to them, and he persuaded Keith to bring in his 'Moog' on that day.

Keith was late. The session was well under way before he turned up, irritated and harassed, with his MiniKorg swathed in acres of bubble wrap, wound round and round till the synth was almost twice its normal size. He'd asked his mum to drive him to Beatbox and then sat with the Korg on his knee, terrified her driving would damage it in some way. He was a nervous wreck by the time he staggered into the studio, holding the Korg out in front of him like a silver tray stacked with delicate porcelain, and it was quite a while before he had the strength to strip it of its bubble

215

wrap and plug it in.

Keith was actually a good keyboard player, but once he'd set up a sound on the Korg he decided that was the end of his contribution.

'You play it,' he told Stuart—who said he didn't know how.

'You should play it,' Stuart insisted. 'It's your Moog.'

'It's not a Moog…' Keith moaned. 'It's a Korg.'

'It's still a Moog, though,' Stuart said, and he tried playing it along with the track.

In the end he managed to persuade Keith to manipulate the sound while they recorded his performance, capturing a series of warblings and bleeps. It sounded great, and even Keith was laughing by the end—having fun.

So one of the tracks had ended up on *Tigermilk*— 'Electronic Renaissance'. Beforehand, the Beatbox recording had been played on Radio Scotland, from a cassette Stuart had sent to Beat Patrol—and while it was being played Stuart had recorded the programme on his cassette recorder at home. The compression the broadcasters had used while they were playing the song made it sound much better to Stuart than his original recording, so he'd spent some time during the mixing of *Tigermilk* with Gregor, trying to replicate the compression setting with Cava's equipment and apply it to his Beatbox recording.

They couldn't quite match it though. Nothing they tried sounded as good as the cassette recorded off the radio. So, in the end, that's what he used—a cassette recording from the radio of the cassette he'd sent to Beat Patrol being played over the airwaves. Gregor recorded it onto the two-inch tape, and it went onto the album.

So Stuart explained to the audience what Keith's contribution to the record had been, and then tried one more time to get Keith to step forward and accept his accreditation. Stuart looked towards the back of the room where some of the Beatbox inmates were standing, guessing that would be the most likely hiding place for Keith.

'Are you there?' Stuart said. 'Put your hand up, Keith.'

And finally, someone who had the full facts at their disposal shouted out over the heads of the crowd, in a matter-of-fact voice,

'He's not here. He's at karate.'

When our set ended, the demarcation between the stage area and the auditorium broke down completely. Members of the band drifted out into the audience, members of the audience strayed onto the stage to talk to Richard or Stevie, who had stayed behind to dismantle their equipment. The students from Stow began the slow task of trying to filter people back up the stairs and out onto the street, and as they quietly coaxed and manoeuvred, they also shouted:

'Take a copy of the album on your way out. They're free.'

I was swept upstairs in the crowd myself, watching people grabbing copies of the album from the picture rail running along to the kitchen, witnessing the presence we had imprinted on Cava gradually disappearing until all that was left of the exhibition of multiples were a few stranded copies dotted here and there—one on a windowsill, one on the floor outside the toilet—a few isolated examples still balancing on the picture rail, like lonely teeth in a gapped smile.

Eventually I found myself out on the sunlit street, amazed that there was still so much daylight after the relative darkness of the studio. The street was crammed with people. Bentinck Street, where Cava is situated, is a residential street, running from the bowling greens in Kelvingrove Park at one end to the Georgian offices on Kelvingrove Street at the other. On both sides of the street are long rows of tenement flats, interrupted by the incongruous domed and pillared building that is Cava. But it's usually a quiet place—there's not much through traffic, either on foot or in cars. On this particular evening it looked as if a spontaneous carnival had suddenly materialised there. Brightly dressed staff from London record companies with blue hair and pink hair, stood in the middle of the road. Laughter and loud voices filled the air. People peered from their windows in the tenements overlooking the street, wondering at this sudden crowd with the large blue squares under their arms.

At one end of the street, carried away by the holiday atmosphere, some people had taken the LPs out of their sleeves and begun flying them down to the other end as if they were frisbees, leaving them scratched or cracked where they landed. Within a few months, the copies that survived would be changing hands for up to £850, but on the evening of the launch party that didn't matter—they were plentiful, free and disposable.

The very next day one appeared in the window of a

charity shop, selling for £1, with no takers for weeks on end. We all agreed it must have been the fastest offloading to a charity shop in history, imagined the donor rushing along first thing in the morning, the moment the shop opened for business, saying, 'Take this. Please. I've already spent one night with it in my house—that's one night too many. Take it.'

Amongst the crowd on the pavements I found David Campbell. He was standing with another friend, looking at his copy of the record. Both of them had kept the vinyl in its sleeve.

'That was a good show,' David said.

They'd both had copies of the albums for a few days, and had listened to them already. 'Richard's playing my drum part on "The State I Am In",' David said. 'That's the same part I recorded in Beatbox.'

As we stood there, Sandy Nelson, who compered the Halt Bar sessions, came and joined us.

'This song "Electronic Renaissance"…' he said, but before he could say anything else David's friend interrupted him.

'Yes! Yes!' he said. 'Yes, that's what I was about to say.'

'That's one of my favourites,' I told them.

'Yes,' David's friend said. 'But it doesn't fit.'

He looked enthusiastically to Sandy, soliciting his confirmation, thinking that was Sandy's point too. 'It doesn't fit in with the rest of the songs, does it?'

Sandy paused for a moment.

'I was just going to say I love it,' he said, and David's friend's excitement faded away.

'It's a good song,' he agreed quietly. 'But it shouldn't

be on this album. No way. It doesn't fit…'

Sandy slapped me on the back and said, 'Good show,' then he got ready to wander off.

'Some crowd,' he said, looking down the street. 'It's kind of surreal. I've never seen so many record company people before.'

I watched him making his way through the crowd, stopping here and there, and something about the whole situation suddenly did seem surreal: the incongruity of the colourful crowd on this usually empty street; the sudden materialisation of so many record industry insiders who always kept themselves aloof and unreachable; the proliferation of the blue cover of *Tigermilk* everywhere you looked; even the bright sunshine and the warm air in a city where it was almost always cold and wet.

I thought of all the disinterest and invisibility we had experienced in all those dark days in Beatbox; of the shows we had played in the art gallery with Alistair and in France just a few weeks earlier, when no one had even noticed us enough to realise they weren't paying attention to what we were doing. I remembered the afternoon I'd walked through the arbour in the park and decided I might try to learn bass—and I felt a bit confused that it had somehow led to me being here, in the middle of all this.

Chris walked past, and said people were making him crazy offers to sign the band to their labels. Bel stood close by, shaking her head and indicating her bemusement when I caught her eye. I had the strange experience of feeling amazed at what Stuart had achieved by writing his songs, while at the same time witnessing at close hand what I'd failed to achieve by writing mine. And yet, somehow, I was now caught up in Stuart's success. My decision to take up the bass had certainly unlocked a door, but it wasn't the one I'd expected it to open.

My thoughts were suddenly interrupted by David, tapping a finger on the cover of his copy of *Tigermilk*.

'What does this mean?' he asked, pointing to the back cover, and the block of text that ran along the top. 'It says here that the band formed over a period of three days in a café. Is that true?'

Very soon, in press releases, the period of time would be shortened from three days to a single night—and the story would stick, like a little myth, for years to come, that Belle and Sebastian had formed in an all-night café.

'We're going to the Art School now,' Chris said, as he brushed past me. 'After-show party.'

I nodded. The crowd had started to move. I stood and watched them streaming past, the record company people moving like a single organism, all having somehow learned the new plan and the new place to be at exactly the same time. Soon the street had gone back to its normal state, empty and quiet, with just the frisbee LPs that littered the road remaining as evidence that anything out of the ordinary had happened.

I went back into the studio to find my bass, then I followed the slow end of the crowd down the lanes towards the Art School, and towards a new place where the contradiction of having failed and succeeded at one and the same time was waiting.

221

Get a Free Copy of *A Century of Elvis*

The Belle and Sebastian song *A Century of Elvis* was based on a longer book of the same name by Stuart David, which is available now for the first time.

To get a free copy, visit:

BookHip.com/KLHKCB

Printed in Great Britain
by Amazon

57038645R00132